War and Peace

Also available in this series:
Creation
Evil

Forthcoming:
God in Action
Science and Religion

Problems in Theology

War and Peace
A Reader

Edited by
Jeff Astley, David Brown and Ann Loades

T&T CLARK
A Continuum imprint
LONDON • NEW YORK

T&T CLARK LTD
A Continuum imprint

The Tower Building
11 York Road
London SE1 7NX, UK

15 East 26th Street
New York, NY 10010
USA

www.continuumbooks.com

British Library Cataloguing-in-Publication Data
A catalogue record for this book is available from the British Library

ISBN 0 567 08973 8 (paperback)
ISBN 0 567 08974 6 (hardback)

Typeset by RefineCatch Limited, Bungay, Suffolk
Printed and bound in Great Britain by MPG Books Ltd, Bodmin, Cornwall

Contents

Preface   vii

Introduction: Reading the readings   1

1 – The context: Theology and ethics   5
*1.1 Christian ethics in context; 1.2 Consequential talk; 1.3 . . . and the
Bible; 1.4 . . . and love; 1.5 Moral objectivity and moral mistakes;
1.6 The Bible and moral norms; 1.7 Sin and idealism; 1.8 Moral
exceptions?; 1.9 Sin and hard choices; 1.10 The theological context
of Christian ethics; 1.11 Working it out in Christ; Topics for
discussion*

2 – Peace and pacifism   27
*2.1 Jesus the pacifist?; 2.2 The context of New Testament teaching;
2.3 The meaning of peace; 2.4 A pacifist Church?; Topics for discussion*

3 – The just war and the nuclear option   43
*3.1 Justifying war; 3.2 Some principles; 3.3 Nuclear war and nuclear
deterrence; 3.4 Judgement and revelation; Topics for discussion*

4 – Holy wars and holy tolerance   62
*4.1 Jihad in Islam; 4.2 The Qur'anic texts; 4.3 Muslim–Christian
relations; 4.4 Islam and peace; 4.5 Arab and Jew; 4.6 Jews and
Christians; 4.7 Toleration and religious freedom; 4.8 Approaching
other faiths; 4.9 Anonymous Christians?; 4.10 Religion and genocide:
the continuing issue; 4.11 Some explanatory notes on Islam; Topics
for discussion*

Acknowledgements   97
Further reading   99
Index of subjects   107
Index of names   109

Preface

Courses in theology and religious studies in universities, colleges and sixth forms are increasingly 'topic-based' or 'problem-based', and usually form part of modular programmes of study for first degrees or AS/A2 level qualifications. Teachers and students often find it difficult to access relevant primary material for the different topics that they have selected to study. Many textbooks are too general to be of more than limited value, and the same is true of selections of readings.

This series of readers in *Problems in Theology* is designed to meet this need by focusing on particular controversial themes and issues. Each volume provides a set of carefully selected readings from primary sources, together with a brief introductory essay, topics for discussion or further study, and a select bibliography. A particular advantage of the format adopted here is that teachers and students can use the material selectively, constructing their own educational pathway through the problem.

The readings chosen for these books have been tested out with undergraduate classes in the University of Durham. Much of this material will also be accessible, however, to sixth form students of religious studies, as well as to those studying theology on ordination courses and in adult education classes.

The editors wish to thank all who have assisted in this project by helping in the selection, referencing and trial-testing of material, by copy-typing and editing the text, or by securing permissions. Particular thanks go to Paul Fletcher, Greta Gleeson, Evelyn Jackson, Declan O'Sullivan and Isabel Wollaston, and to David Webster for writing 'Some Explanatory Notes on Buddhism'.

Notes on the text

The passages are printed (except for omissions, indicated by three or four full stops) as in the original text, with the same spelling, punctuation etc. In most cases, however, notes within the readings have been omitted.

From time to time the editors have added their own explanatory comments. These are printed in italics and enclosed in square brackets.

Introduction

Reading the readings

At any one time, issues of peace and war are matters of immediate and intense concern to large sections of the human population. They are in the background of every major political, social and economic decision and policy. But what have they to do with theology? In this volume we bring together a variety of Christian thinking on these issues, together with some wider religious perspectives on religion and war.

Before debating these issues, however, the Christian theologian needs to face a prior question: What is the relationship between Christianity and moral decision-making? The traditional options for moral theology are a revealed ethic which defines what is right in terms of what God commands; an emphasis on the practice of Christian moral (and spiritual) virtues, many of which either contribute to or partly constitute human flourishing; and the (closely related) 'natural law' theory which argues that unaided human reason can discover what we ought to do on the basis of the natural end or purpose that God has built-in to the human creation (see Readings 1.1, 1.5, 1.6, 1.7, 1.10, 1.11).[1] The second and third positions most easily mesh with the claim that morality must be considered an autonomous domain, the contents of which can be known quite independently of any religious claim. The first perspective in particular tends to focus on moral rules, principles, obligations or 'rights' which express a *deontological* ethic of duty that holds that some human acts as intrinsically right or wrong.[2] By contrast, the *consequentialist* ethic

---

[1] For an overview of the options see, for example, G. R. Dunstan (ed.), *Duty and Discernment*, London, SCM, 1975; Philip L. Quinn and Charles Taliaferro (eds), *A Companion to Philosophy of Religion*, Oxford, Blackwell, 1997, Chs 6, 57, 58 and 59; B. Hoose (ed.), *Christian Ethics: An Introduction*, London, Cassell, 1998; Robin Gill (ed.), *The Cambridge Companion to Christian Ethics*, Cambridge, Cambridge University Press, 2001.

[2] See, for example, chapters 14 and 17 of Peter Singer (ed.), *A Companion to Ethics*, Oxford, Blackwell, 1993, and H. J. Paton, *The Moral Law*, London, Hutchinson, 1948 (this is a translation of Immanuel Kant's classic work, first published in 1785).

of utilitarianism focuses on the effects of our actions, adjudging an action right or wrong in proportion to the balance of the goodness and badness of its actual (or likely) consequences (1.2).[3]

Theologians find little support for a utilitarian ethic in the pages of the Bible (1.3, 1.4; but see also 1.10). But most are also cautious of reading unqualifiable principles of action out of biblical texts (1.6), or from the dictates of conscience (1.5). There is a certain messiness in moral insight, even Christian moral insight; and there is certainly a messiness in our human responses to those insights. This partly results from the inevitable 'sin-filled aspects' of many situations of moral decision-making (Curran, 1.8; see also 1.7). 'Grey-areas', 'hard cases' and 'borderline situations' abound in situations of moral choice. As Martin Luther put it, 'as long as we are here . . . we have to sin' (1.9). Casuistry – the detailed consideration of particular cases – is therefore a necessity in ethical decision-making, and Christian ethics is not exempt from it. Christians are called 'to make God's story my story', and are therefore involved in a moral adventure (1.11). These dimensions are especially important to bear in mind in reflecting on matters of life and death, including those relating to war and peace.

In the chapter of readings entitled 'Peace and pacifism' (Chapter 2), theologians debate the claim that Jesus was a pacifist and that his followers should therefore adopt the same radical view on the morality of war. Absolute pacifists argue that war, or perhaps any violence, can never be justified. They advocate not only (and negatively) non-resistance to evil, but also (and positively) an active, and often self-sacrificial, love. Together these elements are said to possess a potent redemptive power, as exemplified in the crucifixion of Jesus and 'the whole way of life of which it is a symbol' (MacGregor, 2.1; see also Yoder, 2.4).[4]

But this powerful claim for pacifism has not gone unchallenged within the Christian tradition (cf. Ramsey, 2.1). Thus many theologians have pointed out that the New Testament is set in a particular historical context, and was written by a politically-powerless minority who looked beyond history and politics to a kingdom that was not of this world, which they expected God to bring in with power very soon (2.2). Others have argued that pacifists also need to acknowledge the obligations of citizenship and to distance themselves from anarchy (2.4), as well as

---

[3] See, for example, John Stuart Mill, *Utilitarianism*, many editions (first published 1861); J. J. C. Smart and Bernard Williams, *Utiltarianism For and Against*, Cambridge, Cambridge University Press, 1973.

[4] See Isaiah 53:4–12; 1 Peter 2:21–5; Acts 8:32–5; Matthew 5:39.

recognizing that love is no substitute for institutions of justice.[5] Neverthe-less, many would still agree with Stanley Hauerwas that non-violence lies 'at the very heart of our understanding of God'.[6]

While the centrality of peace in the gospel of and about Jesus cannot be denied, the peace of the gospel is one that recognizes divisions and which can itself provoke conflict and confrontation. Jesus brings no easy 'inner peace' and is 'in our terms a singularly unpeaceful person' (Williams, 2.3).

The Christian Church's adoption of a 'just war' morality has seemed to some to be a mistake (1.11), if not a blasphemy, while to others it is no more than a realistic necessity that must mark a more grown-up view of Christian responsibility in the world (1.1). According to just war theory, to be justified in going to war the war must be declared only as a last resort, by a lawful authority, in a just cause and with the right intention, and in circumstances where one may predict both its success and that it inflicts no more harm than those involved would otherwise suffer. In the conduct of a just war non-combatants must not be directly and intention-ally attacked, and any fighting must be proportionate to the intended goals (3.1).

The justification of the use of force to protect *others*, rather than just oneself, is a central concern in debates over the ethics of war (Ramsey, 2.1). Other issues include whether non-combatants should be considered immune from attack, and whether the principle of double effect may be invoked to justify any harmful effects of one's action that were foreseen but unintended (3.2).

There is no doubt that such questions and debates become particularly intense when states consider waging war using nuclear weapons (3.3). The end of the Cold War has not seen an end to the risks of nuclear warfare. A number of questions may be raised here. For example, is every use of nuclear weapons unacceptable under the criteria for a just war (cf. 3.1)? Because of the extent of civilian casualties, is every policy of nuclear deterrence essentially a 'bluff' (see Harries, 3.3)?

The moral relationship between religion and war becomes most fraught, perhaps, where the religious tradition itself seems to endorse warfare as an activity that is commanded by God. Whereas in the rest of this book the readings have concentrated on literature from the Christian religion, here our attention turns to Islam (for background information,

---

[5] See Reinhold Niebuhr, *Moral Man and Immoral Society: A Study in Ethics and Politics*, London, SCM, 1984, Chapter 7.

[6] Stanley Hauerwas, *The Peaceable Kingdom: A Primer in Christian Ethics*, London, SCM, 1984, p. xvii.

see 4.11, Some explanatory notes on Islam). The use of the term *jihad* to justify a 'holy war' may not be true to its roots in the Qur'an (Koran) (4.1), but the Muslim Holy Book does contain encouragements to 'fight for the cause of God, slay and be slain', and promises of divine rewards for the Muslim warrior (4.2). The Jewish Scriptures contain similar injunctions[7] and Christianity too is stained with blood, not least that of Jews and Muslims (see 4.10, Religion and genocide: The continuing issue).

Although war and persecution have sometimes been the outcomes of contact between zealous religious traditions, tolerance and protection have also marked a great part of the intercourse between them. This has certainly been true of much of the history of Islam, even though other faiths were regarded as inferior groups (4.3, 4.4, 4.5). Such considerations readily lead to wider questions of toleration, religious freedom and religious prejudice (4.6, 4.7), and to debates at the common boundary between theology and ethics concerning religious dialogue and the proper attitudes to adopt to other traditions (4.8, 4.9). Although these aspects of the theology of religions may seem somewhat remote from traditional concerns about peace and war, they are inextricably connected in a global political context where religion has to be acknowledged as a highly significant factor.

[7] See, for example, Deuteronomy 7, Joshua 8, Psalm 137.

1   The context

Theology and ethics

1.1 Christian ethics in context

David Brown, 'Christian Ethics: The Contemporary Context', in
C. S. Rodd (ed.), *New Occasions Teach New Duties? Christian
Ethics for Today*, Edinburgh, T & T Clark, 1995, pp. 61–3, 65–70

Roughly speaking, there are three competing accounts of the foundations of ethics, the teleological, the deontological and the consequential.
A brief exploration of the past will set the twentieth century in context.

Philosophically, the teleological is the oldest and finds its most obvious
representatives in the writings of Plato and Aristotle. Derived from the
Greek for 'aim' or 'purpose', it finds ethics' *raison d'être* in the fulfilment
of the given potentialities of human nature. So, for instance, if human
beings are by nature social beings that will necessarily carry with it
certain moral implications. In *The Republic* Plato offered very simple non-
moral examples of what he had in mind. Thus the *telos* of a knife is clearly
to cut well; thereby it achieves its characteristic excellence or *arētē*.
Since *arētē* was translated into Latin as *virtus* (or 'power'), thereby was
born the search for the appropriate powers, virtues or character traits
which together might be said to constitute the flourishing of human
nature. Under the influence of Stoicism and Roman law, the relationship
between potentiality and *telos* came to be expressed in terms of law
('natural law'), and it was this more complicated version which thus
entered Christianity. Because of Protestant stress on the extent of the
Fall and thus on the depravity of human nature, traditionally this
approach has proved much more congenial to Roman Catholic than to
Protestant thinking, but there have been conspicuous exceptions such
as Bishop Butler's *Sermons* in the eighteenth century.

'Law' and 'duty' are characteristic of the second major type of
approach, the deontological (derived from the Greek for 'ought' or 'duty').
Characteristically, this would say that ethics comes to us as an external

demand that bears no intrinsic relation whatsoever to our fulfilment as human beings. The Decalogue with the unconditional character of its laws is often quoted as an example. In the past the Ten Commandments were of course prominently displayed in many a Protestant church. Certainly the greater interest of Protestantism in the Old Testament was one factor that made this approach particularly congenial, but equally important was the notion of the ethical demand as a bolt out of the blue. For ethics and revelation could then be directly paralleled as a transcendent divine summons coming wholly from beyond oneself. Philosophically, this was to receive its most perfect expression in the writings of Immanuel Kant, with his notion of the 'categorical (i.e. unconditional) imperative'. Kant believed that he had available a test for determining duties of 'perfect' (i.e. admitting no exceptions) and duties of 'imperfect' obligation. We were to envisage everyone acting on the maxim upon which we were proposing to proceed; if an incoherent situation was the result (e.g. no one believing promises any more), then a duty of perfect obligation had been identified; if only a conflict within one's will, an imperfect obligation. But few have followed Kant in accepting the existence of such a rational test. Instead appeal has been made to intuition as the proper means of identifying our duties.

Finally, there is consequentialism, the notion that the rightness of an action is determined by its total consequences, the overall balance of good over evil. Its best-known form is of course the utilitarianism of Bentham and John Stuart Mill, that morality is a matter of 'the greatest happiness of the greatest number'. There are certain marked differences from the other two approaches, about which it is important to be clear. Unlike the deontologist, the pure consequentialist denies the intrinsic rightness or wrongness of any particular act; it is always subject to revision should sufficiently deleterious consequences threaten. Again, unlike the teleologist, one is not supposed to look beyond the existing desires and pleasures of those involved to how their life as a whole might be viewed. In other words, like the deontologist but unlike the teleologist, consequentialism is an action rather than character-based theory, and so it is not much interested in what we might become as distinct from what we are.

. . .

[T]hough more often than not seen as competitors, it would seem to me that there is good reason for treating the three major positions I outlined as in some respects complementary. It all depends on what question we are asking. Thus the notion of duties is surely integral to the question of what may be expected of certain stations of life, such as teacher or minister, whereas it would be implausible to analyse all social legislation in terms of a deontological notion such as rights: weighing up the likely consequences of various ways of proceeding would seem exactly the right way of coming to a decision. Yet equally would we not regard someone who has to think on every occasion whether he or she has to tell the truth as a fundamentally flawed individual? Telling the truth must be something that comes naturally out of one's character. So here we have an argument for suggesting that the most basic element of moral education should be grounded teleologically, in particular conceptions of what might constitute the flourishing or fulfilment of human nature. In this context it is interesting to observe that the most important recent book on the use of the Bible in Christian ethics similarly endorses a combination of perspectives (Ogletree, 1984). Consequentialism is absent because so too is any notion of planning. But the Old Testament is rooted in deontology because that is what is most necessary to the successful functioning of a society, while teleology is most characteristic of the New Testament (particularly Matthew's Gospel) because that is what strikes most at the root of human motivation.

THEOLOGICAL RESOURCES

The fact that I have put 'resource' in the plural would have been enough to put an inter-war Protestant generation on its guard. For what I intend to indicate thereby is both Bible and created order, and, as we all know, that generation was quite uncompromising. Thus Bonhoeffer declared in his *Ethics* that the Christian had nothing to learn from secular ethics, while Emil Brunner, despite his well-known confrontation with Barth over natural theology, in *The Divine Imperative* still refuses to acknowledge any role for the non-Christian conscience save that of convicting of sin and drawing the individual to Christ. But were that not bad enough, the problem ran deeper still. For in what seems to me a mistaken desire to ensure that the divine hand is not tied, even within Christianity there is an insistence that no non-provisional ethical judgements may be made. Indeed, so convinced is Barth of this necessity that he even declares in *The Church Dogmatics* that 'the establishment of ethics' was what was promised by the serpent in the Garden of Eden! I hasten to add that in presenting this critique I do not mean to imply that Rome fared any better in this period. So tied had moral theology become to the practical needs of confessors, that in effect it had been reduced to a detailed system of rules justified by tradition or the *magisterium* (the teaching office of the church), or both, frequently without any explicit reference to natural law, far less the Bible.

In the Roman communion all that changed with the Second Vatican Council (1962–65). The largely unsuccessful attempts to reform the sacrament of confession (now known as the sacrament of reconciliation) still further distanced Roman ethical reflection from its traditional context. However, in considering the various factors which helped bring about a transformation in Roman attitudes, one factor which certainly should not be omitted is the influence of that doyen of Roman Catholic moral theologians, Bernard Häring. His 1954 work *The Law of Christ* went through seven editions, and was translated from its original German into many other languages. Though the title may suggest a continuation of the legalistic tradition, there is a significant change of emphasis with the law now understood as the law of the spirit giving life in Christ, the need for conversion stressed, and the call to perfection seen as a summons to all Christians and not just a monastic elite. By the time of his second major work *Free and Faithful in Christ* the transition is complete: law has become entirely secondary to a relationship with Christ.

Appeal to the Bible has thus become as central to modern Roman Catholic ethics as it has traditionally been to the Protestant discussion. Unfortunately, that does nothing to lessen . . . the . . . difficulties . . . As confidence has declined in appealing to specific verses, two alternative trends may be noticed.

The first is resort to identification of derived either general principles or concepts. Paul Ramsey, for instance, makes his *Basic Christian Ethics* revolve round the two notions of love and liberty, while in approaching medical ethics he makes extensive use of the concept of covenant. Another major American writer in the Reformed tradition, James Gustafson, provides a very different perspective by simply relying on the concept of God to critique all existing perspectives as too anthropocentric. However, a major recurring problem has been too easy a conviction that we know what is meant by the concepts concerned. Take love itself. The fact that ethicists as different as Kant and Mill could both claim Jesus as encapsulating their own teaching ought to have provided a salutary warning. Sometimes the naivety of the equation is all too obvious, as in [Joseph] Fletcher's talk of 'an agapeistic calculus' involving 'the greatest amount of neighbour welfare for the largest number of neighbours possible'. But even when faced with sophisticated accounts such as that of Anders Nygren it is not too difficult to detect the extent to which they are merely a projection back into the Bible (and Augustine) of later theological assumptions. What would seem required is a more creative engagement not just with the teaching of the New Testament but also with its contextual challenges and limitations. What response are we to make to the inward-looking character of Matthaean and Johannine love? To what extent might this legitimately be modified by greater attention to the actual practice of Jesus?

Attention to practice is certainly characteristic of the other major trend in contemporary Christian ethics, narrative ethics. Here the basic idea is that of patterning our own lives after the narrative of Jesus' own. Instead of treating the Bible as a compendium of teaching and doctrine, we should use it as the familiar story which through constant repetition helps to pattern our own. Strictly speaking, Liberation theology is not narrative theology, but it clearly displays affinities, with its repeated rehearsal of the events of the Exodus as a model for understanding the summons to contemporary Christians in Latin America to engage in confrontation with the powers that be, in order to liberate the poor and the oppressed. Though this has normally been conceived in non-violent terms, it still stands at a considerable distance from the non-violence which Hauerwas draws from the narrative of Jesus under the influence of the Mennonite theologian, John Howard Yoder. Here there is a call to be a community set apart, living the ethics of Jesus, but bearing no responsibility to transform the world, because there can be no shared ethics between Christian and non-Christian. The church is there to invite and cajole, rather than to permeate the society in which it is set.

Once again, this approach seems to me to raise acute issues of contextuality. Was not Jesus' life so unique that it is hard to draw conclusions so directly for our own? Thus, was not Jesus addressing a situation of complete powerlessness, in which his followers had neither responsibility for the ordering of society nor the ability to effect change by force (events repeatedly demonstrated by the pointlessness of resistance to Rome)? But from that we need not conclude that the message would have been the same in a situation of responsible power. In his life and teaching Jesus clearly demonstrated what to do in love when one's own private interests are threatened, but the post-Constantine church (rightly, in my view) gave a very different answer when it saw third party interests affected. Love was still the underlying assumption, but it was now a love required to act in defence of the threatened other, and it is one thing to abandon one's own interests; quite another to sacrifice a weak and vulnerable other. And so the just war theory was born.

Given the fact that Hauerwas taught for many years in a Roman Catholic university, it is not surprising that his writings provide a number of parallels with Catholic thinking. None the less on this question of dialogue with the world he clearly retains the more traditional Protestant perspective. Yet he is now far from typical. For, if Rome has moved, so too has Protestantism. This is well illustrated by what is perhaps the most extensive Protestant analysis of Christian ethics since the Reformation, Helmut Thielicke's multi-volumed *Theological Ethics*. Like Barth he lost his post under the Nazis, but unlike Barth those traumatic years generated a profound revolution in his ethical thinking. Law and Gospel are not seen as antitheses, but as essential constant partners, with Reformation theology acknowledged as inadequate in its failure to do proper justice to the extent to which the will of God is already embodied in the orders of creation, and thus amenable to dialogue between believer and non-believer. Accordingly, he does not hesitate to draw detailed ethical conclusions in a way that would have been inconceivable for Barth in his concern for divine freedom. Yet Thielicke does offer an important qualification in his notion of 'the borderline situation', where in typical Lutheran fashion he argues that where a conflict of goods is concerned there may be no necessarily right answer . . .

1.2 Consequential talk

Richard Higginson, *Dilemmas: A Christian Approach to Moral Decision Making*, London, Hodder & Stoughton, 1988, pp. 35–42

There is little doubt that in the modern, increasingly secularised West, the consequentialist approach to moral decision-making has become increasingly dominant. This does not of course mean that rules have now been discounted, or dispensed with. But life has become less governed by rules, certainly by absolute rules; one could say that the status of many rules has been relativised. And whenever a case is being made for keeping a rule or ignoring it, the likelihood is that evaluation of consequences will feature prominently, if not exclusively, in the argument.

. . .

Talk of consequences inevitably raises the questions: 'What sort of consequences?' 'What are to count as good consequences and what as bad?' The philosophical idea which, implicitly or explicitly, has dominated consequentialist thinking in the West is Utilitarianism. According to this school of thought, consequences should be calculated in terms of utility, or usefulness. But again we have to ask a further question: 'What sort of usefulness?' and the answer given is in terms of whether actions produce pain or pleasure, suffering or happiness.

Utilitarianism in one form or another has been around for a long time, but as a clearly and consciously articulated philosophy it is reckoned to have started with Jeremy Bentham (1748–1832). Bentham reacted strongly against the rule-based morality of his age by which certain actions were considered to be *intrinsically* right or wrong. He dismissed the concepts which were used to justify such thinking (like 'man's moral sense', 'eternal and immutable rules of right', or 'a law of nature') as empty and meaningless. To him they represented an evasion of human responsibility to provide a single, scientifically objective standard of morality.

Bentham's *An Introduction to the Principles of Morals and Legislation* begins thus:

> Nature has placed mankind under the governance of two sovereign masters, pain and pleasure. It is for them alone to point out what we ought to do, as well as to determine what we shall do.

> . . .

Bentham was adamant that all types of pleasure and pain could be measured on the same scale. In other words, they can be compared *quantitatively* because there is no *qualitative* difference between them. He once said that 'quantity of pleasure being equal, push-pin is as good as poetry'. Actually Bentham had little time for poetry, criticising it as misrepresentation (one can see that it ran counter to his calculating out-look) and this is one area where John Stuart Mill (1806–73), the most important of his utilitarian successors, parted company with him.

> . . .

He found Bentham 'one-eyed' in a number of respects. Thus Mill, who was lifted from a period of deep depression by his discovery of Words-worth, appreciated poetry and more generally the arts in a way that Bentham never did. He emphasised the pleasure of freedom (a quality surprisingly missing from Bentham's list) and wrote an important essay 'On Liberty'. Most importantly, his method of calculating pleasures was not merely quantitative. He regarded intellectual pleasures as qualita-tively superior to physical ones, arguing that the pleasures of the intellect, the imagination and a clear conscience are more valuable and desirable than those of man's animal nature.

> It is better to be a human being dissatisfied than a pig satisfied; better to be Socrates dissatisfied than a fool satisfied. And if the fool

or the pig are of a different opinion, it is because they only know their side of the question.

He is assuming that the educated person, who has been both educated and uneducated, who has experienced the pleasures of both body and mind, would definitely opt for the pleasures associated with his education. Problems and pains the latter may also bring, but the benefits, in Mill's view, more than compensate. Indeed, they are such as to rank on a different qualitative scale altogether.

. . .

Utilitarian thinking is perhaps most explicit today when we talk of costs-benefits analysis. Like Bentham, we recognise that some courses of action can bring pleasure *and* pain, desirable consequences and undesirable ones. Like him, we attempt to analyse the costs and the benefits, whether we are contemplating the effects of closing a school, resiting a factory, or redistributing resources in the health service. Again and again we try to arrange things so that human happiness is maximised or, where circumstances dictate for the worse, so that human suffering is minimised.

Nevertheless, it would be quite misleading to say that all moral judgments are of this costs-benefits type. Consequentialist thinking in general and utilitarian assumptions in particular are widespread, but they do not rule the roost completely. There is another sort of moral language in use which does not speak principally, if at all, in terms of consequences.

. . .

Specific rules about how human beings should and should not be treated often flow from recognition of human rights. And though Utilitarianism is not incompatible with strongly-held rules, the language of rights tends to invest these rules with a greater aura of inviolability. Because the human person is regarded in a special light – even, in some versions, as someone *sacred* – anything which might be construed as 'violating' him is to be avoided at all costs. According to this way of thinking, ethics should be construed not in consequentialist terms but deontological ones. The word *deontology* is derived from the Greek for necessary ('what ought to be'). Some states of being simply ought to be, others ought not. The overriding stress is on doing one's *duty*. Certain attitudes and actions invariably constitute one's duty; they find expression in laws (e.g., do not commit adultery), principles (faithfulness in marriage) or institutions (marriage itself). Violation of these laws, principles or institutions would amount to dereliction of one's duty.

1.3 . . . and the Bible

Thomas W. Ogletree, *The Use of the Bible in Christian Ethics*, Oxford, Blackwell, 1984, pp. 204–5

I have not offered much comment on the virtual absence of consequentialist thinking in the biblical materials. . . . In my initial discussion of consequentialist thought, I noted its link with the distinctive experiences of modern societies. Consequentialism is a mode of inquiry and reflection which can come into its own only when the people of a society have considerable confidence in their ability to predict and shape the future course of world events. Insofar as it has gained a position of dominance in nineteenth- and twentieth-century thought, it is because of its special congruence with high-technology civilization. If anything, modern society has exaggerated the human capacity to manage the course of events, at least from the standpoint of its utopian projections if not in its actual practice. What implications do these experiences and attitudes have for contemporary attempts to appropriate biblical faith into constructive ethical thought?

Modern societies can no longer function effectively without a good deal of 'rational' direction and control based on considerable technical knowledge of geographic, ecological, economic, social, and political processes. Even when this knowledge is distorted by ideological biases and is inadequate to the complexities of the actual world, it provides critical reference points without which large-scale social policies could scarcely be conceived, let alone implemented. Contemporary social ethics must address these realities in some fashion, which means it must come to grips with consequentialist thinking.

If this judgment is sound, then a biblically informed ethic must find suitable ways to develop the possible import of biblical understandings for a world which requires the assessment of policies and courses of action in terms of values likely to be promoted by their probable outcomes. Drawing upon central themes in biblical faith, we have need of a fully articulated account of values which can guide our analyses of policy options. Such an account will have to attend to many factors which scarcely appear as matters of moral concern to the biblical authors: global scarcity, population pressures, ecological vulnerability, the monetary system, international trade and corporate

development, urban planning. At a minimum it will have the burden
of challenging the tendency of consequentialist thought to reduce
the values pertinent to decision-making to economic and political
factors.

What a Christian ethic must surely resist is the impulse to translate all
moral understandings into consequentialist terms. We must be concerned about consequences, but our assessment of probable
consequences and their associated values must at every point be con-
strained and ordered by perfectionist and deontological considerations
[*that is, considerations concerned with the full realization of virtue or
moral excellence, or with notions of obligation expressed in abstract principles and rules*]. Before giving ourselves enthusiastically to grand
designs which may or may not eventually be realized, we have need to
attend carefully to the basic requisites of communal and social existence
as we understand them, and to keep in view the conditions pertinent to
moral and spiritual growth.

1.4 . . . and love

David Brown, *Choices: Ethics and the Christian,* **Oxford,
Blackwell, 1983, pp. 43–5**

[I]t certainly cannot be claimed that Christ acted in the best utilitarian
way in his life on earth, in the sense that he tried to achieve the maximum
good of which he was capable. For, quantitatively, he could probably
have achieved far more by being in an influential position on the staff of
Pontius Pilate or Herod. Again there is no record of him seeking out the
sick and healing as many of them as he possibly could. All that can be
said is that with each individual he encountered and entered into some
sort of relationship, he saw that particular person's need and met it.
Equally, when one considers the interpretation of the term 'neighbour', in
the command to love our neighbour as ourself, which Christ gives in his
parable of the Good Samaritan (Luke 10:25ff), one finds no demand for
generalized, impartial benevolence. The Good Samaritan acts only
for the benefit of the one wounded traveller he encountered. He does not,
for instance, set up a fund to help other travellers suffering similar mis-
fortunes on the road. So, strictly speaking, the parable justifies the
inference, not that one's neighbour is anyone, but rather anyone in need
whom one personally encounters or with whom one enters into some sort
of relation. This is not to deny the challenge for love to become more
extensive in its concerns. It is simply to point out that, according to

Jesus, the failure of love is at its most fundamental only where personal encounter or responsibility is involved.

. . .

From the time of Thomas Aquinas onwards there is no doubt that both the psychological and moral necessity of realizing that love is a relation to *specific* individuals is fully taken into account. Aquinas himself does not hesitate to underline the fact that, the greater the number of connections we have with another person, the more love can and ought to bind us to them:

> We love them more because we love them in more ways. For those who are not connected with us are loved only with the friendship of charity, but towards those connected with us, other kinds of friendship come into play, dictated by the kind of tie that binds us together . . . So, to love someone because he is a kinsman, or connected to us, or is a fellow citizen, or because of any other lawful reason that accords with the end of charity, is an act that can be commanded by charity. (*Summa Theologiae*, 2a, 2ae, 26, 7)

Likewise, Bishop Butler protests against the equation of love, and indeed of all virtue, with a generalized benevolence. He suggests that, even if God is a utilitarian, he has so made our nature that we must not be.

> The fact then appears to be, that we are so constituted so as to condemn falsehood, unprovoked violence, injustice, and to approve benevolence to some preferably to others, abstracted from all consideration, which conduct is likeliest to produce an overbalance of happiness or misery. And therefore, were the Author of Nature to propose nothing to himself as an end but the production of happiness, were his moral character merely that of benevolence; yet ours is not so. Upon that supposition indeed the only reason of his giving us the above-mentioned approbation of benevolence to some persons rather than others, and disapprobation of falsehood, unprovoked violence, and injustice, must be that he foresaw this constitution of our nature would produce more happiness, than forming us with a temper of more general benevolence. (*Fifteen Sermons*, ed. T. A. Roberts, p. 152)

1.5 Moral objectivity and moral mistakes

F. C. Copleston, *Aquinas*, Harmondsworth, Penguin, 1955, pp. 226–8

Aquinas believed that actions which are contrary to the natural moral law are not wrong simply because God prohibits them: they are prohibited by God because they are wrong.

. . .

Believing in a human nature which is constant Aquinas was led to postulate an unchangeable moral law; but some of the precepts which he regarded as forming part of its content have not been regarded by many people in the past and are not now regarded by many people as moral precepts at all. Is it not reasonable to conclude that Aquinas simply canonized, as it were, the moral convictions and standards of his time or at least of the society to which he belonged?

This is a far-reaching problem and I must content myself with making the following relevant point, namely that differences in moral convictions do not by themselves constitute a disproof of the theory that there is an unchangeable moral law. For there might be an unchangeable moral law and at the same time varying degrees of insight into the content of this law, these differences being explicable in terms of the influence of a variety of empirical factors. To use the value-language, there might be objective and absolute values and at the same time different degrees of insight into these values. I do not mean to imply either that the existence of an unchanging moral law was for Aquinas an uncertain hypothesis or that the explicability of differences in moral conviction on the theory that there is such a law proves of itself that the theory is true. My point is that differences of opinion about moral precepts and moral values do not constitute a proof of the relativist position.

. . .

Conscience may be erroneous, whether through our own fault or through some cause for which we are not responsible. And if our conscience tells us that we ought to perform a particular act, it is our moral duty to perform it. 'Every conscience, whether it is right or wrong, whether it concerns things evil in themselves or things morally indifferent, obliges us to act in such a way that he who acts against his conscience sins' (*Quodlibetum*, 3, 27). This does not mean that there is no such thing as right reason and no such thing as an objectively correct moral conscience; but ignorance and mistakes are possible in moral matters, and the nearer we come to particulars the greater is the field for error.

1.6 The Bible and moral norms

Bruce Birch and Larry Rasmussen, 'The Use of the Bible in Christian Ethics', in Ronald P. Hamel and Kenneth R. Himes, OFM (eds), *Introduction to Christian Ethics: A Reader,* **New York, Paulist, 1989, pp. 326–8**

A more *direct* influence upon moral norms can take a variety of forms. The Bible might be regarded, as it has often been, as the source of a revealed norm of its own.

. . .

Sometimes the biblical materials work differently, however. Rather than supplying a distinctive, revealed norm of their own, or a cluster of them, they work so as to transform the norms already common to the human enterprise. Thus an Augustine or an Aquinas was not simply accommodating or being hypocritical in affirming certain pagan norms and asserting their ethical integrity even while these norms needed transformation in light of biblical revelation. The norms, then, might originate in many quarters of the human experience. The biblical materials rank, illumine, and transform them.

Our contention is that the Bible can and ought to be a source of moral norms for the Christian life. At the same time, and for almost any given decision, it will not function as the sole source of norms. Nor should it.

The role of biblically influenced norms will be a double one. Negatively, some otherwise plausible norms will be ruled out. Positively, a different set will be confirmed or 'authorized'.

. . .

The biblical materials might not only provide straight-forward prescriptions, however. They might also be the source of guidelines *for locating the burden of proof* on a given moral issue and choice.

War and revolution, for example, or even a case of assault on a normally peaceful neighborhood street, can force that moral turbulence which questions whether or not there is a justifiable taking of human life. In the heat of battle that question will be answered one way or another, with little or no reflection. But in a previous time of relative calm, or a later one, the person may ask for aid in making up his or her mind. The biblical materials can help locate the burden of proof. In this case, the scriptures mandate that the general rule be one against the taking of life. If there is any exception to be made that has moral integrity, then it must be one which at least begins with a non-violent bearing as the normal and normative one for the Christian. That is, the use of lethal violence is *not on the same level of choice* with non-violence, or even non-lethal violence. Its use, if allowed at all, requires a special justification.

1.7 Sin and idealism

Charles E. Curran, *Directions in Fundamental Moral Theology*, Notre Dame, Indiana, University of Notre Dame Press, 1985, pp. 43–5

The encyclical *Pacem in Terris* [*from Pope John XXIII in 1963*] well illustrates the failure of Roman Catholic theology to realize the existence of sin in the world. A theology which does not come to grips with the existence of sin will tend to be dangerously naive and romantically optimistic – dangers which are to some extent present in *Pacem in Terris*. The very title of the encyclical indicates the penchant for a too one-sidedly optimistic understanding.

. . .

As human beings and Christians we are called upon to work for peace, and can and should do much more than is now being done. The fullness of peace in all its ramifications, however, will always elude our grasp. The very title of Pope John's encyclical thus appears somewhat distorted in the light of the full Christian vision of reality. The 1983 pastoral letter of the American bishops has a more appropriate title – *The Challenge of Peace: God's Promise and Our Response*.

   In the Introduction Pope John explains the methodology which he will employ in the encyclical. The creator of the world has imprinted in human hearts an order which conscience reveals to us and enjoins us to obey. The laws governing the relationships between human beings and states are to be found in human nature where the Parent of all things wrote them. In the final introductory paragraph the Pope explains that these laws teach citizens how to conduct their mutual dealings, show how the relationships between citizens and public authority should be regulated, indicate how states should deal with one another, and finally manifest how individual citizens, states and the community of all people should act towards each other. These four considerations are the skeleton outline of the encyclical which then develops the teaching on each of these points in the four main parts of the encyclical.

In a certain sense what Pope John says is true, but there is something else in the heart of human beings – disorder or what Christians have called sin. A glance at the world around us only too easily confirms the existence of these disorders even in the four areas in which the encyclical stresses the existence of order. The vision of the papal teaching is somewhat unreal if it does not take into account this sinful aspect of reality. There is definitely order and the possibility for a greater order in the world, but there remains the obstacle of sin which any realistic ethic must consider. One perhaps could argue that Pope John was talking about the ideal and urging people to live up to that ideal without descending into the very concrete ways in which this is to be accomplished. Perhaps there is some validity in such a defense of *Pacem in Terris*, but if the encyclical is to serve as a realistic guide for life in our society, then it must at least recognize the persistent reality of sin and how sin will affect our world and our actions. One must always talk about the ideal towards which all must strive, but a realistic assessment of the obstacles is necessary for the completeness of the teaching.

Whereas some forms of Protestant theology have overemphasized the reality of sin, Catholic theology generally has not given enough importance to sin. In ethics the natural law theory tended to forget sin.

1.8 Moral exceptions?

Charles E. Curran, *Directions in Fundamental Moral Theology*, Notre Dame, Indiana, University of Notre Dame Press, 1985, pp. 177–8

McCormick himself maintains that the existing laws or norms accepted in Catholic moral theology have ultimately come about by refining the principle that killing is wrong except where there is a proportionate reason. Exceptions have been made in this general norm for proportionate reasons (self-defense, killing in war, etc.) without endangering the value to be preserved by the norm itself. Now one might attempt to push the question one step further – can exceptions be made in the now accepted norms of no direct killing of the innocent and no active euthanasia which could allow for some exceptions without entailing all the evil consequences that McCormick fears if one no longer accepts the existing distinctions?

In the case of directly killing noncombatants in war I am in basic agreement with McCormick's fears, but in the case of directly killing the innocent, it might be possible to make some very limited exceptions. Consider a case which was proposed by Williams. A foreigner comes across a scene where a tyrannical military captain is prepared to shoot a group of villagers taken at random to discourage other protesters in the village and bring about loyalty to the existing government. The captain offers the foreigner the privilege of killing one of the villagers with the promise that he himself will then let the others go free. The presuppositions are that the captain will do as he threatens and there is absolutely no other way to save the villagers or any number of them. Is it not possible to acknowledge some exception clause for hard cases like this without necessarily involving the many long-range consequences feared by McCormick? Could one not accept the rule – directly killing the innocent is wrong except in those cases where one is forced into a situation in which there is certitude that this is the only way a far greater number of innocent persons can be saved? Such a restricted exception clause could allow such killing in a few cases and still maintain the general principle of not killing innocent people in almost all situations. Here it is necessary to insist on the sin-filled aspects of the situation and on the certitude that one has that this is the only way in which a far greater number of innocent persons can be saved. Such a condition is rarely present and impossible in the complex situation of warfare and the direct killing of noncombatants.

1.9 Sin and hard choices

Richard Higginson, *Dilemmas: A Christian Approach to Moral Decision Making*, London, Hodder & Stoughton, 1988, pp. 129–32, 134–6

In 1981 a charge of murder was brought against the paediatrician Leonard Arthur for [injecting] a three-day-old baby suffering from Down's Syndrome with a fatal dose of a powerful drug. During the course of his trial and the accompanying public debate, much reference was made to the 'grey area' in which doctors who treat handicapped babies have to make difficult decisions.

. . .

There are theological counterparts to this talk of grey areas. In this chapter I shall draw attention to the work of Helmut Thielicke (1908–86),

Professor of Theology for many years at Hamburg, and author (between 1945 and 1964) of a vast *Theological Ethics*. Fundamental to his ethical thought is his understanding of the *borderline situation*; and borderline situations, for Thielicke, are essentially problematical situations where the Christian has freedom to choose, but only between different alternatives all of which are marked by sin.

In viewing ethical decision-making in this way, Thielicke reveals some characteristically Lutheran presuppositions; Luther's theology is of central importance to him. The first presupposition is the Christian's *freedom* . . . The second, somewhat contrasting presupposition is the pervasiveness of human sin. The Christian is *simul justus et peccator* (at the same time a righteous man and a sinner). For Lutherans, this phrase operates on various different levels of meaning.

On one level, *simul justus et peccator* expresses the very heart of Christian existence: man is a sinner, through and through, but at the same time he is deemed righteous, and therefore made righteous, in the sight of God. . . . But *simul justus et peccator* also describes the situation of the Christian living in a fallen world where involvement in the God-given orders of existence invariably involves sin, and where there are often no pure alternatives available. Sometimes Luther expressed impatience with an attitude of undue scrupulosity towards sin. In a letter to his fellow-Reformer Philip Melanchthon, he wrote thus:

> If you are a preacher of grace, then preach a true and not a fictitious grace; if grace is true, you must bear a true and not a fictitious sin. God does not save people who are only fictitious sinners. Be a sinner and sin boldly, but believe and rejoice in Christ even more boldly, for he is victorious over sin, death and the world. As long as we are here (in this world) we have to sin. This life is not the dwelling-place of righteousness, but, as Peter says, we look for new heavens and a new earth in which righteousness dwells. (Letter to Melanchthon, 1 August 1521)

The phrase 'sin boldly, but believe and rejoice in Christ even more boldly' is often quoted by Thielicke, and for him sums up what should be the Christian's attitude when faced by a difficult moral dilemma. The Christian should acknowledge the sinfulness which pertains to either option, but nevertheless feel emboldened to act, confessing his sin and secure in the promise of God's forgiveness.

. . .

Thielicke cites many vivid examples from the Nazi period, when he was a member of the Confessing Church which offered some resistance to Hitler. He points out how in the attempt to mitigate the worst effects of Nazism, resort to devious means was often necessary. For instance, complicated webs of forgery and deceit were often constructed to save the lives of individual Jews. Thielicke believes that such action was right: those who helped the Jews to escape actually 'found their true existence'. Yet because of the illegality and deception involved, Thielicke thinks that this assistance was not devoid of guilt.

. . .

On the other hand, feigned co-operation can involve an intolerable measure of participation in evil practices, e.g., in preparation for war, mass executions or persecution of minorities. It may thus run the risk of helping to validate and perpetuate a disreputable system. Decision here must be left to the individual conscience, and individuals will doubtless decide differently. It may even make sense for two persons working side by side to respond differently, one making the outward demonstration of opposition and the other working to save the situation from within.

. . .

A Lutheran theologian who worked from inside the Nazi system actually to overthrow the regime was, of course, Dietrich Bonhoeffer; and in him – as with Thielicke – we see a readiness to confess sin even about what he regarded as a justified course of action. Involvement in the plan to kill Hitler grew out of the responsibility he felt towards the people both of Germany and of Europe, but it was still for him a matter of getting his hands *dirty*. In place both of 'an irresponsible lack of scruple' and a 'self-tormenting punctiliousness' which never leads to action, Bonhoeffer spoke of the discovery of free responsibility which is the mark of civil courage:

> It depends on a God who demands responsible action in a bold venture of faith, and who promises forgiveness and consolation to the man who becomes a sinner in that venture. (*Letters and Papers from Prison*, ET London, SCM, 1971, p. 6)

This is very much the spirit of Luther's 'sin boldly, but believe even more boldly and rejoice in Christ'.

1.10 The theological context of Christian ethics

Stanley Hauerwas, *The Peaceable Kingdom: A Primer in Christian Ethics*, London, SCM, 1984, pp. 21–3

The concentration on obligations and rules as morally primary ignores the fact that action descriptions gain their intelligibility from the role they play in a community's history and therefore for individuals in that community. When 'acts' are abstracted from that history, the moral self cannot help but appear as an unconnected series of actions lacking continuity and unity.

Perhaps it is because we sense so deeply the need for unity, for integrity, that we take for granted one of the other assumptions shared by deontological and teleological [*here used as equivalent to 'consequentialist'*] theories. Each assumes that order and coherence for morality as an institution, and thus for the individual, can only be secured by establishing a single fundamental principle as a criterion from which the various rules and obligations are derived and ranked. Utilitarianism perhaps presents the clearest example of this because of the simplicity of the formula 'the greatest good for the greatest number,' but deontological systems often seek a similar overriding principle. Such a principle, even if it is highly formal, seems necessary since both theories assume that any apparent moral conflict must ultimately be resolved in the light of some more general principle. As a result neither theory can countenance the idea of moral tragedy – that is, the possibility of irresolvable moral conflict.

Yet we live in a world of such conflicts and we cannot negotiate that world unless we are trained with virtues sufficient to sustain us in that endeavor. But the attempt to develop an unqualified ethic, with the attending stress on rules and obligations, has resulted in a failure to stress exactly those virtues we need to live in such a world.

. . .

No less distorting for Christian ethics is the assumption that we must choose between teleological and deontological theories of obligation. Of course, there are aspects of the Christian tradition that seem to fit into either theory. Those inclined toward the deontological option tend to emphasize God's commanding presence or the necessity of covenant fidelity. Those more attracted to the teleological alternative often stress love as the overriding aspect of Christian ethics. There is no reason to deny that the biblical record and Christian tradition manifest deontological and teleological tendencies, but it is mistaken to assume that Christian ethics requires us to choose either alternative or some combination of the two. For when we do so we inevitably tend to abstract the Christian 'ethic' from its rationale by subordinating theological convictions to prior formal patterns of ethical argument.

For example, many who are convinced that ethics is primarily a matter of rules, assume that Christian ethics must have its primary source in the Ten Commandments or the Sermon on the Mount. While both are extremely significant for Christian ethical thinking, they are unintelligible when treated as sets of rules justifiable in themselves. The Decalogue is part of the covenant of God with Israel. Divorced from that covenant it makes no sense. God does indeed command obedience, but our God is the God who 'brought you out of the land of Egypt, out of the house of bondage' (Deut. 5:6). Because of this action the demand 'You shall have no other god before me' can be made. So too, the commands not to kill, not to commit adultery, and not to steal necessarily make sense only within the particularity of the story of God's dealing with Israel.

1.11 Working it out in Christ

Stanley Hauerwas, *The Peaceable Kingdom: A Primer in Christian Ethics,* **London, SCM, 1984, pp. 130–4**

Though currently casuistry [*the detailed consideration of specific cases*] is regarded with a good deal of suspicion as a minimalist endeavor to evade some of the more onerous obligations of a legalistic ethic, no community can or should try to avoid developing a tradition of moral testing embodying the wisdom of that community concerning sets of issues peculiar to its nature. The question is not whether to have or not to have casuistry, but what kind we should have. This is particularly the case among Christians, since the very nature of our convictions makes problematic any account of a self-centered decision-making process.

. . .

Casuistry, at least in a Christian context, is not just a possibility but a necessity, because it provides the means by which we learn to check our own particular rendering of the story of God with that of our community. The church not only is, but must be, a 'community of moral discourse' – that is, a community that sustains a rigorous analysis of the implications of its commitments across generations as it faces new challenges and situations. For as I suggested above, as a people, often we do not understand the implications of the narrative that gives us our being. The church is that community pledged constantly to work out and test the implications of the story of God, as known through Israel and Jesus Christ, for its common life as well as the life of the world.

There is no assurance that this 'working out' will always be faithful to the kind of discipleship required by Jesus. For example, it may well be that the development of the 'just war' theory, which was certainly an imaginative attempt to maintain the gospel's commitments to forgiveness and peacemaking and yet respond to the Christian's increasing responsibility to wider society, was a mistake.

. . .

The church is the pioneer in displaying the implications of God's kingdom of peace brought in Jesus Christ. She does so by a relentless questioning of every aspect of her life as we learn slowly what it means to be a people of peace in every aspect of our existence. The 'prohibitions' that become part of that community's life must not become minimalistic rules. Rather they should charge the imagination of the community and individuals to chart new forms of response necessary to being a people of peace in a violent world.

For example, it is particularly important that such a community maintain the connection between truthfulness and nonviolence. For violence is often the result of the lies and half-truths we perpetrate on one another. And when the falsehood is discovered it becomes the seed of resentment and hate, inviting retaliation and violence that often takes the form of another lie. Therefore the church must be a community that demands truthfulness in all its dealings with one another and the world. Of course, it is often hard to know what the truth is and that too must be admitted truthfully.

. . .

Christians may well appear to those 'outside' our community to be overscrupulous about some matters – e.g., lying, sexual fidelity, just arrangements – but we are such because we have learned through long centuries how quickly we can lose the habits necessary to being a people of peace. Of course those habits can also become ossified if we assume their very presence is sufficient to ensure our peacefulness. It cannot be forgotten that casuistry is required, and it is required as a community activity, because morality always deals with those matters that can be other. Our moral convictions depend on the experience and wisdom of a people who have been and continue to be on a journey of discovery charted by the God we have come to know through Israel and the life, death, and resurrection of Christ. The judgments of those people about such matters as truth-telling, divorce, life-taking, and so on reflect and must be tested by the stories of Israel and Jesus. But such testing is not simply a deduction from a text to actions, but the testing by others who have also been formed by that story and have perhaps discovered more appropriate ways to understand and shape our practices, habits, and choices.

In this sense, all members of the church should understand themselves to be involved in a moral adventure for which they have an important role. For we are each charged to seek constantly a better understanding of what it means to make God's story my story. Our lives literally enrich one another, as we learn the full power of that story only by seeing it displayed in others' lives. We must, therefore, always remain open to the challenge of others, who may well teach us about how to be truthful in ways we had not anticipated.

Topics for discussion

1 What are the principal arguments for and against (a) a consequentialist morality, and (b) a deontological with its stress on specific duties and obligations? Must one always make the same choice, or are they both relevant but in different contexts, or even in the same context?

2 What difference might your choice make to the conduct of a war? Or to the example mentioned by Curran?

3 What contribution should the Bible make to Christian ethics? Is its role for the Christian supplementary to what is already given in conscience, or should it function as his/her sole controlling guide? What implications does your answer have for the development of a Christian ethic of war and peace?

4 How plausible is the notion of a universal moral law available to all, whether believer or not, through conscience, i.e., the notion of natural law?

5 How persuasive do you find the arguments for necessary exceptions to moral rules, based on the ubiquity of sin, for example, in Curran or Thielicke? If one allows such exceptions, is there any clear way of distinguishing between a dubious 'compromise with evil' and a 'tragic necessity'?

6 How important is it to place individual decision-making in the wider context of the Christian community? To what extent could this preclude dialogue with the non-Christian?

2   Peace and pacifism

2.1 Jesus the pacifist?

G. H. C. MacGregor, *The New Testament Basis of Pacifism,*
London, James Clarke, 1936, pp. 92–7

In reply to the charge that Christian Pacifism, by exalting the Gospel of absolute love, dethrones the conception of law and justice taken over by Jesus himself from the Old Testament 'Law' and 'Prophets', and thereby undermines the very foundations of righteousness, we may now note the following points in greater detail:

(1) Jesus' new and distinctive ethic, *and in particular the definitely pacifist features in it*, is specifically stated by himself to have as its aim not the 'destruction' but the 'fulfilment' of the Law. The whole section begins with the statement: 'Think not that I came to destroy the law or the prophets: I came not to destroy, but to fulfil' (Matt. 5:17). And at the end of the section we have the 'non-resistance' and 'love-your-enemy' sayings as the culminating illustrations of what Jesus means by 'fulfilling the law'. To 'fulfil the law' in Jesus' thought evidently means to 'give the full content' to the older conception of Law, 'to draw out its underlying intention', 'to make explicit that which hitherto has been only implicit'. Just how His pacifist ethic achieves this we shall discuss in a moment. Meantime it is important to note that Jesus Himself, though definitely claiming to modify and in a sense even to supersede the Law, just as definitely denies that He is 'destroying' it.

Paul, too, frankly admits that in large measure the Gospel, when rightly understood, has superseded the Law – but always in the sense not of 'destroying' the Law, but of accomplishing that at which the Law aimed, but failed to achieve. We are guilty of 'heresy', not when with Paul himself we recognize and insist upon this kind of supersession of the Law by the Gospel, but when like Marcion and Dr Temple himself we set the way of justice and the way of love in so sharp an antithesis as to suggest that when we choose the one we necessarily 'destroy' the other. Neither Jesus' teaching nor Paul's means that justice has been dethroned by love; it does mean that all human relationships must ultimately be based on the Gospel of love; that justice truly 'fulfilled' is an outcome of love, rather than love a mere by-product of justice; that if we aim at love we shall establish justice by the way; that we can in fact secure justice only when we aim primarily not at it, but at the love out of which it springs. Paul feels the same about peace: like love it is one of the 'fruits of the Spirit', the reward of a whole way of life, to be attained not by aiming at 'peace' alone, but as one of the 'by-products of a larger quest'.

(2) Before we ask how the pacifist ethic of Jesus does actually thus 'fulfil' or, to use more modern language, 'sublimate' the conception of law and righteousness, it will be well to recall what was said above about 'affirming the moral order'. Jesus does not think, as do we too often with our academic ways of thought, of a 'moral order' in the abstract, which evil, again in the abstract, has invaded, and which has to be 'vindicated' by resistance to evil as a thing *per se*. That is to use legal and political analogies, and results in the misconception that God is concerned with abstract 'law' rather than with persons, and that His chief end is to 'vindicate the moral order of the universe', and to 'uphold His own righteousness', rather than to fulfil His purpose of redemption towards mankind. Jesus on the other hand is dealing always, not with such an abstract 'moral order', but with a world consisting of persons in relation to one another and to God; and in such a world justice can be truly 'vindicated', and God's own righteousness 'upheld', not by the mere restraint and punishment of evil, but only by making evil persons see the sinfulness of their ways, through the employment of a redemptive method which will change the evil will, and restore right personal relationships, 'so making peace' (Eph. 2:15). For peace in the international sphere also depends upon something much more than the restraining of an 'aggressor' or the vindication of a 'righteous cause'. Peace depends upon right relations between persons, upon mutual confidence in the common honesty, upon co-operation by all for the service of all, upon something far deeper than mere justice in the abstract, however ingeniously worked out by international 'formulae'. There can be no peace in any sphere at all which is not also what Paul calls 'the peace of God which surpasses all human ingenuity' (Phil. 4:7).

(3) How, then, does Jesus' pacifist ethic redeem the will from evil to good, restore right personal relationships, and thus truly 'fulfil' and sublimate the Law? It does so because it offers, not merely negative passivity in the face of wrong, but an alternative, positive, and redemptive

method of overcoming evil, which renders all violent and punitive methods obsolete. The injunction to non-resistance, which is so often taken to represent the whole pacifist ethic, is immediately followed by the positive commandment of all-embracing love. Retributive justice, which merely checks and punishes evil, is supplanted by active and self-sacrificial love, which redeems and changes the evil will, so 'vindicating righteousness' in the only true sense of the word, and thereby 'fulfilling the Law'. This, and not mere non-resistance, must always be the foundation of the Pacifist position when adopted on specifically Christian grounds. For the Christian, if he renounces war, will do so, not because he denies that to react against evil by way of war may sometimes be better than not to react at all, but because he is convinced that to use such methods is equivalent to trying to cast out devils by Beelzebub the prince of devils, and must stultify at the outset every effort to make credible and effective this alternative and positive method of sacrificial and redemptive love, to which as a disciple of the Crucified he is called.

It is unnecessary to repeat here . . . how Jesus in His own Person and by His own example proved again and again the power of active love to overcome the evil in men's lives. And in the Cross the method of non-resistance finds its complete and final illustration, and the redemptive way of sacrificial love its perfect example. For Jesus deliberately willed to endure the Cross rather than prove false to His chosen redemptive way, believing that He and His could overcome the evil in men only by being willing to suffer to the uttermost rather than betray that way; and at Calvary we see Him laying down life rather than take it, in His own Person meeting the wickedness of violent men, Himself bearing sin's utmost penalty, the Just for the unjust, and yet overcoming that sin by the power of active, forgiving love. It is important, too, to remember that Jesus never sought to avoid the application of these principles because that way might lead to suffering and danger for others as well as for Himself. He never promised immunity even from death itself to those who accepted his way: 'If any man would come after me, let him . . . take up his cross, and follow me' (Mark 8:34). When He 'steadfastly set His face to go to Jerusalem' (Lk. 9:51), He risked His followers' lives as well as His own. If He had been swayed by considerations of their safety, there would have been no Cross. But there would also have been no Resurrection, and no releasing into the world of the redemptive power of love.

What is it that gives to the Cross, and to the whole way of life of which it is the symbol, this unique 'redemptive' power, that is the power to defeat evil by changing the evil will and winning it to good? I know of no finer statement than this:

> God's purpose is to win men's hearts to Himself . . . Obviously there is only one method of winning such a victory when methods of force are ruled out, and that is simply to love; to love so passionately, so utterly, that even the most brutal and seemingly triumphant violence of sin leaves it still love, unchanged except in the increasing agony of its disappointed desire to bless and to redeem. The only qualification for victory required of love is that it should be able to endure its most shattering defeat and yet still remain love. If it does that, it has still got the whip hand; for in its very weakness of defeat it has within it the invincible strength of remaining itself, and it will yet win its victory. As someone has said, 'You cannot defeat defeat' . . . Let men take every advantage of the seeming weakness of love, let them bruise and batter and seek utterly to smash it, as they did at the Cross; but let it still remain love, and in the end they will have to give up, and look upon what their hands have done, and break down in its presence. At some time or other the very weakness of love will cut them to the centre of their being with more power than a two-edged sword – only it will be spiritual power. I am sure that is so, human hearts being what they are. The weakness of a God of love is stronger than men. (H. H. Farmer, *Things not Seen*, London, Nisbet, 1927, pp. 32–3)

Paul Ramsey, *Basic Christian Ethics*, London, SCM, 1953, pp. 169–71

Whether the whip Jesus used in driving the money-changers out of the Temple was plaited of straw or of leather, whether he applied it to animals or to men, whether the decisive factor that day was the force of his own powerful personality justifiably indignant on behalf of a righteous cause or the threatening multitude of people gathered in Jerusalem who forestalled the immediate use of the Temple police, in any case some form of resistance was raised that day not only against perverse practices but also against the men who engaged in them. Force does not become any less resistant because of its 'spirituality', or resistance wrong to a greater degree because it takes material form. Circumstances similar to those which warranted a change from Jesus' announced ethic of non-resistance to any manner of resistance he may have used in cleansing the Temple may not only permit but even on occasion require Christian love to adopt physical methods of resistance.

A recent study of Christian attitudes toward war and peace puts the issue of a preferential ethic of protection in terms of Jesus' story of the Good Samaritan: 'And now arises one of the unanswerable "ifs" of literary history. What would Jesus have made the Samaritan do while the robbers were still at their fell work?' In answering this question, the author, apparently without any hesitation, substitutes Jesus' personal ethic in relation to a single neighbor, and all his apocalyptically derived strenuous teachings having to do with this simple situation, for what might have been his ethic in multilateral relation to two or more neighbors. He writes, 'The protection of one life would have seemed to Jesus no excuse at all for taking the life of another, even a robber.' Surely the most that can be said is that quite plainly the protection of *his own* life did not seem to Jesus any excuse for ceasing to express non-resisting love for another. It may be 'there is no evidence for the suggestion that Jesus would have had him wield his traveler's sword.' Still, in the rudiments of preferential ethics to be found in Jesus' attitude toward the perpetrators of injustice there is some suggestion that he *might*, at least no decisive evidence that he would *not*, have approved such action. We perhaps should not go to the other extreme so far as to say, 'When I try to imagine what would have happened had Jesus come upon the scene a little earlier than the Good Samaritan, I find it more natural to suppose that he would have helped the traveler in his struggle with the thieves than that he would have waited until the man was injured and the thieves departed before coming to his aid.' To say the least this would have been a different ethical situation from the one pictured in the story or from an attack by thieves upon Jesus himself. The difference is precisely that non-resisting, unself-defensive love must determine its responsibility in the one case toward more than one neighbor, in the other simply toward the neighbor or 'the enemy' when injurious consequences of the decision will fall upon the agent himself alone.

To express love at all in some situations one must seem to deny it. Jesus said: 'If any man smite you on one cheek turn the other also'; here the situation is relatively simple – you and your enemy. But Jesus did not say: 'If any man smite one of your friends, lead him to another friend that he may smite *him* also.' Not only is it clear that Jesus could have made no such statement, but also that he would have felt that the involvement of the interests of others (that is, others besides one's self and one's enemy) transformed the whole moral situation and placed our obligations with respect to it in a radically different light. (A quotation from the New Testament scholar, John

Knox, from his essay in H. P. van Duser (ed.), *The Christian Answer*, Scribners, 1945, p. 173)

2.2 The context of New Testament teaching

Victor Paul Furnish, 'War and Peace in the New Testament', *Interpretation*, XXXVIII, 4, 1984, pp. 363–4, 379

It is not difficult to find books and articles in which the New Testament is examined for its teaching about war and peace. Too often, however, these studies have paid little or no attention to several factors which make this an especially difficult topic to handle.

1. In contrast with the writings of the Hebrew Bible, those of the New Testament were all written within a period of approximately one hundred years, about AD 50–150. Even when due account is taken of the fact that earlier Christian traditions (e.g., those about Jesus) have been employed by the New Testament writers, the period is lengthened by no more than twenty years. Although one must reckon with important changes in the political situations and issues with which Christians had to deal even during the course of this ten or twelve decade span, one will not expect to find the major changes in situation and outlook which can be charted in the history of Israel.

2. Jesus' life and ministry, and the subsequent emergence of the Christian movement (including all of the writings which came to be included in the New Testament), took place within an empire that the Romans had made relatively secure and free from any serious threat of invasion. Frontier battles there were (notably, with the Parthians) and civil strife, but not the kind of major 'international' conflicts reflected in certain parts of the Hebrew Bible.

3. The religious community from which the New Testament writings came, unlike ancient Israel, had never had a national history of its own and had no experience of political or military power. The earliest believers constituted a sectarian minority within Judaism, which was itself an ethnic and religious minority within the Roman Empire, without effective political power.

4. Finally, and of decisive importance, the New Testament writings came from a religious movement which understood itself to be in the world but not of it. Whereas Israel's faith was oriented to God's action in its own national history (even when it looked forward to a future fulfillment), the church's faith was oriented to what it perceived God had already accomplished in Jesus the Christ (even as it also looked forward

to a future fulfillment). Parallels may be drawn – and the early church itself drew them – between faith in Yahweh's saving power as manifested in the Exodus event and faith in God's saving power as manifested in Jesus' death and resurrection. Yet the fact remains that the church understood the Christ event to have inaugurated not just a new phase of history, but a whole new age. Whereas Israel closely associated its history as the people of God with 'salvation history,' the church – at least in the earliest periods of its life – regarded all historical existence, including its own, as radically qualified by God's saving work in Christ.

. . .

That the church made no attempt, this early, to ask in what ways its gospel was relevant to the issue of war and peace was due partly to political conditions in general, partly to the church's status as a minority movement largely without access to political power, and partly to the kind of eschatological hope to which it clung. However, the gospel to which the New Testament bears witness by no means precludes a concern for such larger 'social issues.' Indeed, it demands a concern for them, since it affirms that God's coming rule is sovereign, and that it already graces and claims the present, however short or extended this may be.

2.3 The meaning of peace

Rowan Williams, *The Truce of God*, London, Collins, 1983, pp. 28–30, 65–9

In the early Middle Ages, the great Burgundian monastery of Cluny sponsored and encouraged an experiment in conciliation among its feudal neighbours – half-civilized landlords in a state of more or less endemic war with each other. The arrangement, known as 'the truce of God', was that all hostilities should be restricted to three days in the week (Monday to Wednesday). Of course, this was never observed for any length of time with much consistency; and in retrospect its mixture of naïve earnestness and cynicism is rather funny (very characteristic of the Church, somehow . . .). But it is more than a comical bit of mediaeval eccentricity. Behind it lay the recognition that for baptized Christians, sharers in the Body of Christ, to be in a state of war with one another was horrible and ridiculous. The mild ludicrousness of the response pales, however, in comparison with the absurdity of people, who could in principle kneel side by side to share the communion of Christ's body and blood, also planning revengeful slaughter against each other.

Mediaeval Christians seem very odd to most of us today, and nothing is helped by romanticizing them in a G. K. Chesterton style. But there are points at which they really do challenge us very sharply. They had a certain instinctive sense that symbols were not a matter simply of decoration, but both declared and actualized certain policies for meaningful living. Thus there were, for them, situations in which they could not treat actions as 'just' symbolic. When King Henry II refused to give the kiss of peace at Mass to Thomas Becket, he was a better theologian than he knew. He recognized that giving the kiss would not only suggest that he *was* at peace with Thomas (which he was not) but would also commit him to *seeking* peace (which he did not want to do). He knew well enough that he had no intention of giving the symbol room to work; and so, rightly and honestly, he sinned boldly and refused it.

Imagine for a moment a far from impossible situation: an East German Christian attending a parish communion service somewhere in Britain. [*Williams is writing at a time when East Germany was still a Communist state, and its Church persecuted.*] Would anyone be so rude and unwelcoming as not to shake hands with him at the Peace? Of course not. Very well; but what are we expressing and what are we seeking in such an act? How far do we in fact intend to 'give room' to this symbol?

I know that this is an unfair and strained analogy, and I use it only as a reminder that questions about international reconciliation are not always abstract and far away. Recently, Dr Peter Matheson of Edinburgh produced, for the Scottish Methodist Peace and Justice Centre, 'Ninety-five Theses' on nuclear warfare; the third of these very disturbing and sharply worded propositions was: 'Christ's Church does not cease at the Oder–Neisse Line' [*used to symbolise the former division between Communist and Western Europe*]. He goes on to argue that, if the Church is a new humanity, a universal royal priesthood, its wavering commitment and uncertain voice on the nuclear issue is 'un-churching the Church' (thesis 32). How can a church that claims to be catholic – for all humanity – settle down with a situation in which its central symbols of reconciliation are put in question by the fact that those who celebrate them are divided by abiding suspicion, hostility, and planned aggression? If it does so, it is undermining its own deepest reality. For the Church is itself a symbol – of the 'catholic' love of God for his creation, the adaptability of his love to each and every creature; and so it is also a symbol of the truth that, because of the nature of this love, human beings have a common destiny. They are meant to be one, not in some super-personal collectivity or organism, but one in the patterns of their growth, the goals towards which they move. Each and every person, as the object of God's compassion and grace, has received a call to grow into free, conscious and responsible love. In this sense, there is *one* human future in God's purposes, and its unity is crystallized in the *one* story of a particular person, in his living and dying. That one life of full and mature compassion, acceptance and understanding is our future. Christ is the goal to which we move.

. . .

When the Jesus of the fourth gospel proclaims to his disciples, 'Peace I leave with you; my peace I give to you, not as the world gives do I give to you' (John 14:27), the assurance most Christians tend to hear in these words is of a peace more secure and lasting than any the world can offer. But this is not precisely what is said: 'not as the world gives' suggests both that the peace in question is not of the same sort as anything we habitually call peace, and that the giving itself is of a new and different order. What is offered and the way it is offered are alike a challenge to the world's peace.

In all strands of the gospel tradition, Jesus is not a figure readily associated with peace in the sense of visible harmony. He provokes conflict and confrontation, and says truly enough that he brings not peace but a sword (Matthew 10:34), that he comes to kindle a fire on the earth (Luke 12:49). In response to him, men and women discover and decide the basic orientation of their thoughts and wants: they are *judged*, and thus they unearth in themselves all kinds of hidden divisions and disunities. It may be true to say that through Jesus the world can discover a fundamental unity, a community of destiny; but it would be a fatal reduction of the Gospel to say that Jesus's work is simply the revelation of universal brotherhood. As has so often been said, it is hard to understand why anyone purveying such a bland message should ever be crucified. To preach a *natural* unity between all human beings as something simply to be seen and acknowledged takes us back to the fantasies of a natural state of peace and passive 'interlocking' . . . Before human unity can mean anything, we need to see why it is not obvious – how situations have been created in which there is no community of interest and purpose between people. We need to grasp in penitence how we have co-operated in fragmenting a world called to unity. And this does not mean scraping away divisions and distinctions to find an equality 'under the skin', but committing ourselves *in* our diversity to the creation of new and mutually enriching patterns of interaction. If our historical actions have created a divided world, our historical actions, our choice and speech and imagination, must create a world of positive mutuality.

And this precipitates the new and grave division of which Jesus speaks so sombrely – the division between the penitent and the impenitent, between those who see the world's calling to community and those content with fragmentation. The tragic impasse is that those compelled by the vision of community are driven by this vision to rupture many of the forms of communal living they are already involved in, because the uncritical acceptance of these forms implies an acceptance of the corrupt and divisive wider structures of which they are a part – or simply because these forms cannot tolerate the presence within them of a wider vision. The New Testament is haunted by the breach with the synagogue; Paul in Romans struggles to see how this destructive and bitter schism can be a stage in the creation of a wider 'peace' in God's mercy. Jesus himself, in the passages already quoted, is poignantly aware of the threat to the treasured harmony of family life. To receive Christ's peace is to share Jesus's own position as a sign of contradiction, and to be drawn into a course of action that seems constantly to be deepening rather than healing the gulfs of understanding in the human world.

Can we somehow ease this dilemma by appealing to some gift of 'inner' peace which provides the resources for dealing with the confrontations of the world outside? Is Christ's peace not the peace, the authority and confidence, which characterized Jesus as a person? Certainly it is true that when we talk about Christ's peace we must mean some kind of share in Jesus's life or experience; but insofar as we can say anything with confidence about what kind of a man Jesus was, there seems at first little to reassure us. The gospels do not present us with a figure marked by any evident serenity – rather with someone in important respects scarred by his own divisive role and painfully aware of the costliness of what he is doing. He has to bear the knowledge that he will cause the destruction of the peace of Jerusalem (Luke 19:41–44); worse still, his calling of Judas turns out to be a call to catastrophe and despair, to self-damnation (Mark 14:21). He cannot spare men and women the effects of his presence; and he does not hold back his tears.

So he is a sign of contradiction not least because he is himself so vulnerable to the contradiction he provokes. The crisis, the dividedness, seems to run through his own person. Spiritually as well as materially, it seems that the Son of Man has no place to lay his head, but that he must carry in himself both the compulsion of his calling, the unanswerable command to be the Father's Son in all things and to force the Kingdom closer, and the cold clarity of knowing that his presence as the Son and the herald of the Kingdom is for some an occasion of sin and self-destruction. Without his presence, some might have lived and died in their innocence (John 15:22). He must sustain the urgent and transfiguring vision of an ultimate mercy at last made plain and the knowledge that he cannot make it so plain that all will see it. His irony, his imagination, his anger, his despair, his many-layered and even anarchic wit, all of them stem from the struggle to make visible to all what is to him so visible that it needs no description and escapes all description; and when he cries out against the obstinate stupidity of his hearers, it is because he has exhausted the resources of language and picture to no avail in trying to communicate to people what lies in front of their noses. He is at once eloquent and inarticulate; and at last, confronted with the rational politics of Caiaphas, he falls silent. 'If I tell you, you will not believe; and if I ask you, you will not answer' (Luke 22:67–68).

This is not peace as we see it. Jesus is a man profoundly not at home with his world and his contemporaries, and so in our terms a singularly unpeaceful person. And his isolation is not somehow smoothed over by a warming private conviction that all is well: his faith is a weightier and a darker thing than that. There is no peace for him on earth, in the present order. His life is directed towards the coming Kingdom – which is an order of peace quite different from the 'quiet life' we may long for. Jesus's miracles are often seen as 'signs of the Kingdom', clues to the fact that it is at the door; and they are miracles of freeing from bondage, healing, feeding, and life-giving. They speak of a realm where the Father's will is done by the removal of what actively damages and limits human dignity. And the recurring image of the Kingdom's joy is the feast of the royal Messiah, the king's banquet thrown open to paupers, cripples, rogues and vagabonds.

There is peace at the banquet not because nothing is happening but because people are reconciled, accepted sufficiently to relate to each other in love, gift and enjoyment. They are at home with each other and their host; they are at peace and they are *making* peace. But the food at the messianic feast, the supply of nourishment which makes it possible, is the love and welcome of the host. And when we in the present crisis, the moving world of time, anticipate the feast, we do so by remembering just how that love took final shape for us. Our food is the crucifixion: a body broken.

2.4 A pacifist church?

John Howard Yoder, *'The Challenge of Peace*: A Historic Peace
Church Perspective', in Charles J. Reid, Jr (ed.), *Peace in a Nuclear
Age: The Bishops' Pastoral Letter in Perspective*, Washington, DC,
The Catholic University of America Press, 1986, pp. 273, 288–9

Among the many perspectives for both affirming and challenging criticism that *The Challenge of Peace* [*A Pastoral Letter on war and peace of
the Conference of American Catholic Bishops*] so fruitfully provokes, my
task is to identify those questions arising from the particular perspective
of the nonviolent minorities within Christian history, who have recurrently
challenged the dominant vision of justified violence that took over Christian moral thought in the fourth century. By 'historic peace churches' are
traditionally designated three denominations present in North America:
the Mennonites from the 16th century, the Quakers from the 17th, the
Church of the Brethren from the 18th. Fuller historical accuracy would
add others; some older, like the Waldenses from the 12th century or the
Czech Brethren from the 15th, and some younger like the Churches of
Christ from the 19th, and from our own century early Pentecostalism, the
Kimbanguist community in Zaire, and the Mukyokai in Japan.

The right of the peace churches to be heard is not based on any success they might have recorded in building world peace or in performing
works of mercy, or even in merely surviving: The reason for them to be
heard is only that what they say is on the subject to which the letter
speaks and that they have been saying it for a long time.

The phrase 'nonviolent minorities' that I first used reaches beyond
sectarian Protestantism or the historic peace churches. For centuries
the same moral position was prescribed for Franciscans, for pilgrims in
penitence, for practically all priests, and for serfs.

Nor should we commit ourselves to any specific interpretation of the
relation between minority status and nonviolence. Is it that the nonviolent
position is not assumed by many people because it is costly: 'It is a
narrow gate and a hard road that leads to life, and only a few find it'? Or is
it the other way around? Is it that only the exclusion of these people from
social domination provided them the exemption or the luxury of leaving
coercive social management to others? We need posit no one answer to
that. Nor must one understand 'minority' numerically. In any tyrannical
society, the powerless people are a numerical majority.

. . .

It is always somewhat unfair to read a document for what it fails to say: Often the hazards of redaction and compression do not reflect any intentional or even unconscious selectivity. It is, however, still notable that paragraphs 39–54, dealing with Jesus, remain hopelessly general. The themes of the proclamation of the reign of God, of resurrection and forgiveness are clear. The notion that the law is fulfilled, which is the central theme of Matthew 5, itself identifiable on literary critical grounds as the core ethical catechism of the Gospel, is not accentuated. Neither is the way in which three of the six contrasts in the chapter have been centred on radicalizing the prohibition of killing, the end of retaliation, and radicalizing love of the neighbor into love of the enemy. The love of the enemy is referred to but the radicality of the Gospel writer who framed that text to make us see it as more than just an all-inclusive love is avoided. Paragraph 37 says we are to love as Jesus loved us: The Gospel is far more radical in that it says we are to love enemies because God does.

A second significant lacuna in the New Testament interpretation is that Jesus is spoken of only as the proclaimer of the coming kingdom or as the teacher of an ideal morality. That sets aside weighty dimensions of the lived humanity of Jesus the social leader:

1. That he was discharging a messianic mission, defining in his career a response to the challenge to be a zealot liberator. Rejecting quietism he agreed to be a liberator: yet he rejected righteous revolutionary violence as well.
2. The sweeping portrayal by the entire New Testament of the sacrifice of Jesus as a paradigm for the life of the disciple. The witness of the New Testament to the kingdom of peace is thereby flattened into a long-range social idealism, the goal of a better social reality to be worked toward by whatever means we find reasonable. Jesus is flattened into a teacher of a slightly more generous and slightly more demanding moral idealism, but not different in substance from other moral idealisms.
3. The fusion of Atonement and ethics in the Cross that is *at once* divine transaction and human obedience, unique achievement, and general paradigm.

George Weigel, *Tranquillitas Ordinis: The Present Failure and Future Promise of American Catholic Thought on War and Peace*, New York, Oxford University Press, 1987, pp. 344–5

The theology of peace must think harder about *pacifism* than has been the case in American Catholicism since Vatican II. The legitimacy of the pacifist conscience for individual Catholics has been made plain in the teachings of the Council, of recent popes, of the American bishops, and of many Catholic theologians. That 'Catholic pacifist' is not an oxymoron [*a contradiction in terms*] is no longer in dispute. But recognizing the legitimacy of a personal pacifist commitment opens, rather than closes, the needed debate. How shall the individual pacifist conscience function within the Church? How shall the pacifist conscience address the wider political community? Gordon Zahn's call for a nonsectarian Catholic pacifism taking responsibility for political action in history is welcome. But toward what ends, measured against what standards, shall that distinctive Catholic pacifism work?

A pacifism contributing to the reclamation and development of the classic Catholic heritage would have several distinguishing characteristics. It would challenge the selectivity by which some pacifists mount radical critiques of American military strategies and programs, but turn a blind eye to revolutionary violence in the Third World. The American bishops rejected such a challenge during their final debate over the 1983 pastoral letter on war and peace; one commentator called Bishop John O'Connor's call for consistency 'snide.' It is not, of course, snide at all. A pacifism true to its own standards should have mounted the challenge of its own accord.

American Catholic pacifism would also, on principle, eschew military prescriptions. The pacifist conscience cannot reject the resort to armed force in the defense of rights and then offer counsel on the force structure of the American military. Pacifism only corrupts its distinctive message and mars the quality of its witness when it enters the arena of prudential judgment where, as 'The Challenge of Peace' teaches, other criteria drawn from just-war analysis and its moral economy of the use of armed force must apply. Pacifists who wish to enter the policy arena must consciously adopt standards of judgment distinct from those they choose to apply in their own lives.

American Catholic pacifism could still play an important role in the policy debate by focusing on the development of international legal and political institutions for prosecuting conflict without the use or threat of mass violence. A pacifism that wishes to enter the arena of responsibility for history would see law and democratic governance as the most wide-spread, effective means for resolving conflict in ways congruent with pacifist insights and values. American Catholic pacifism has not been distinguished by its thoughtfulness on these questions. Primary attention has been focused on resistance to American military programs. And when pacifists discuss alternatives to war, themes drawn from the U.N.'s Third World caucus tend to dominate.

Yet why should not an American Catholic pacifism serious about democratic political community as a means for resolving conflict be at the forefront of work to reform international agencies like UNESCO? Why should not American Catholic pacifism take the lead in challenging the gross politicization of the U.N. General Assembly, and the obscenity of acts such as the identification of Zionism with racism? There is no rea-son, in principle, why pacifists should not develop the most trenchant critique of present international organizations, and then point the way to their reform (or replacement). The obstacles to such a pacifist contribu-tion to the reclamation and development of the Catholic heritage lie, not in principled pacifism *per se*, but in the deterioration of principled paci-fism through political understandings derived from sources external (and, in many cases, hostile) to the pacifist conscience.

Principled American Catholic pacifism would reject fundamentalist or literalist approaches to Scripture in the moral debate over war and peace, security and freedom. Principled pacifism would also make a distinctive contribution to the Church's pastoral ministry on questions of personal conscience, war, and civic responsibility. To urge draft resistance as a means for stripping the gears of the American 'military machine' is not an act of pacifist witness; it is anarchism (at best; sedition at worst). Yet the question of the draft does bring issues of war and peace down to the sharpest level of personal moral choice. The Church thus has an important pastoral ministry to those faced with involuntary (or voluntary) military service. Principled pacifists (with nonpacifists, of course) could take up the ministry of draft counseling. But in doing so, they would stress not only the prerogatives of personal conscience, but the obligations of citizenship in a society whose laws protect the right of conscientious objection. This has not been a consistent theme in Ameri-can Catholic pacifism. Yet the reasons why are, again, not indigenous to the principled pacifist conscience. The themes dominating the rhetoric of contemporary draft registration 'resistance' are largely drawn from Vietnam-era New Left teachings about the corruption of American soci-ety and its necessarily corrupt intervention in the world.

Pacifists serious about alternatives to violence in the resolution of conflict – that is, pacifists serious about democratic law and governance – should be prominent among those challenging the idea that personal conscientious objection to military service can be uncoupled from the moral demands of citizenship. Conscientious objection without a parallel commitment to civic responsibility – without a concrete expression of one's commitment to work for the peace of political community – is not pacifism, but anarchism (however confused and muddled). Principled pacifism would bring this teaching into the life of Church and society and, in doing so, would contribute to the reclamation and development of the heritage of *tranquillitas ordinis* in a sound theology and politics of peace.

Topics for discussion

1 What should we understand by the term 'peace'? What light do the Bible and the Christian tradition throw upon its meaning?
2 What difficulties are there in the way of appealing to the New Testament as a basis for pacifism, and how easily may they be overcome?
3 To what extent should the Crucifixion be taken as the model for all Christian behaviour?
4 Is conflict as inevitable for the pacifist as for the non-pacifist? Is the pacifist sometimes duty-bound to seek conflict?
5 Is pacifism an end in itself, or is it adopted as a means to an end? If the latter, is it sometimes the case that the end could be better achieved by resort to other means, including perhaps the use of force?
6 How would you explain the concentration of the pacifist tradition in certain specific denominations? Is the notion of a Catholic or an Anglican pacifist a contradiction in terms?
7 What features might distinguish Christian pacifism from other accounts of pacifism?

3 The just war and the nuclear option

3.1 Justifying war

Richard Harries, *Christianity and War in a Nuclear Age*, London, Mowbray, 1986, pp. 63–8

During the first two centuries of the Church's existence most Christians were reluctant, for a variety of reasons, to join the Roman army. When Constantine became Emperor, much changed, and by the year 410 the army had become a closed shop for Christians. The Church blessed God for the *Pax Romana* and saw in it the fulfilment of the prophecies of peace contained in the Old Testament. It is true that some Christians on the edge of the empire did not see it in these terms, notably the Donatists [*a schismatic Christian group*] in North Africa. But the vast majority saw the empire as providential and had no difficulty supporting it by prayer and the sword. Some Christians now regard what happened under Constantine as the great betrayal, the time when the Church sold its soul and, in return for its position of privilege, gave state power a religious sanction.

The matter can, however, be looked at very differently, as a time when the Church grew up and assumed its fair share of responsibility for the ordering of the common life we all share. No doubt this was not possible when the Church was a small, persecuted and heavenward-looking sect. But, when under Constantine it had the opportunity, which it took, of sharing in the exercise of coercive power and being tainted with the associated guilt, it showed a proper maturity. For we live in society, and society needs political control. It is not for the Church which cares for the conditions under which men live and which serves a master who did not scruple to mix with both soldiers and collaborators, to disassociate itself from those who exercise power. The Church is indeed concerned with the city of God. But on this earth it shares with all men the conditions of life without which there can be no earthly pilgrimage. As St Augustine put it:

Thus, the heavenly City, so long as it is wayfaring on earth, not only makes use of earthly peace but fosters and actively pursues along with other human beings a common platform in regard to all that concerns our purely human life . . . (*City of God*, bk. XIX, ch. 17)

It was during the fourth and fifth centuries, particularly under the influence of Augustine, but also Ambrose who baptized him, that the Church began to consider more carefully the conditions under which it might be morally right to go to war. This has now come to be called the 'just war' tradition. It is not a static body of thought but has been subject to continuous modification and development over the centuries in response to different historical circumstances. Nevertheless, there is a remarkable degree of continuity in the principles that have been taught. As now received by us, the tradition may be divided into two main parts. First, the moral considerations that arise when deciding whether or not to go to war (*ius ad bellum* [*just rules preparatory to war*]). Secondly, the morality of the conduct of the war (*ius in bello* [*just rules in war*]).

The main conditions that must be fulfilled for a war to be called just are as follows.

1. It must be declared by supreme authority. When two citizens have a dispute they can go to a court that will arbitrate between them. If one of them is dissatisfied by the judgement he can appeal against it right up to the highest court in the land, which will then make a final decision. But there is no supreme international authority able both to make and to enforce a decision. Although all countries pay lip service to the United Nations, if a matter of vital national interest is in dispute and the UN is failing to resolve the matter in a way that is satisfactory, the government of a country that feels aggrieved may well feel, on moral grounds, that force has to be used, even though in so doing it violates the charter. Below the level of government, disputes can be resolved; in the end, by government itself. Between governments there is not, at the moment, any effective arbitration. So governments retain the right to defend themselves; which is usually stretched in practice to the right to defend their vital interests and those of their allies.

2. The cause must be just. According to the UN Charter, there is now only one just cause, and that is the right to defend oneself if attacked. The 'just war' tradition, however, never limited just cause to wars of defence only. There could be a just war of offence to recover territory that had been lost, or more generally to right a grievous wrong. The

British war to recover the Falklands, for example: is it to be seen as a war of defence, or as a war to recover territory that had been lost? More controversially, the United States invasion of Grenada could not be ruled out *per se* by the Just War tradition.

3. War must be a last resort. Every effort must have been made to resolve the crisis by peaceful means.
4. The expected war must not inflict more harm than would otherwise be suffered. (The principle of proportion.)
5. There must be a reasonable chance of success. This is, in fact, an extension of the previous condition. Luther, for example, said that it was absurd and immoral to go to war against the Turk, with a much smaller, ill-equipped army, in which defeat would be likely; for this would simply bring about even greater suffering.
6. The war must be fought with the right intention. It must be waged with a view to establishing a just peace.

The two main moral conditions that must be observed in the conduct of the war (*ius in bello*) are as follows.

1. Non-combatants must not be the direct and intentional object of attack.
2. An attack on a particular target must be proportionate: i.e. if Britain had used nuclear weapons against the Argentinian mainland in order to recapture the Falklands, most people would have judged this disproportionate.

It is obvious that every one of these conditions raises many questions and there has been much debate over the centuries as to what exactly each of them means. For example, there have been disputes as to how likely success has to appear before a war can be held to be just. Does it have to appear near certain? Or just probable? Or will an even chance of victory be enough? Furthermore, what counts as success? Revolutionary wars, for example, do not count on big military victories. Revolutionary war is primarily a political struggle, and what counts as success is staying in the field, being enough of a nuisance, until the political victory has been won. Again, it has been doubted whether these conditions apply in a war of defence. If it is a life or death struggle even to survive, in the face of a direct attack, some hold that it is the moral thing to do to fight even if the odds against the victory are overwhelming.

. . .

. . . some more general points about the 'just war' tradition, in view of the still widespread misunderstandings about it that abound.

First, it is not primarily a way of justifying war. No doubt that is the use to which it has most often been put. But it is no less meant to be a check on going to war. Its basic assumption is that war is a very terrible thing and can only be justified for the most serious reasons. It asks whether the reason is really serious enough. It assumes that there is a *prima facie* case against going to war, and puts the burden of proof on those who claim that in this particular instance it can be justified.

Secondly, it is sometimes said today that the 'just war' tradition has been rendered obsolete by the advent of nuclear weapons. It no longer applies. Nothing could be further from the truth. For the very judgement that some might make, for example that any use of nuclear weapons would be disproportionate and could not be justified by any conceivable good, is a judgement using one of the canons of the 'just war' tradition. There are two ways in which a person can make a judgement that a particular war is immoral. He can do so on pacifist grounds; for the reason that all war is immoral. Or he can give reasons why this particular war, or kind of warfare, is immoral. Those reasons will be drawn from the long tradition of thought on this subject that goes under the name of the 'just war' tradition.

Thirdly, although the 'just war' tradition has in the main been developed by Christian theologians, there is nothing distinctively Christian about it. The origin of the tradition lies with the Greeks, many years before Christ. From the time of Grotius in the sixteenth century, the tradition became just as much part of international law as it was of moral theology. In its early stages, *ius in bello* owed much to the professional ethic of the knightly class and, in its later stages, it became enshrined not only in international law but in the military manuals of most countries in the world. So, although the tradition of moral thinking by theologians is clearly discernable, it built upon, responded to, and fed into, the work of people whose prime interest was in law or the practical business of fighting. For some, the fact that there is nothing distinctively Christian about the 'just war' tradition rules it out from the start. And some of the grave suspicion that it arouses today amongst Christians is because they hanker after a distinctively Christian stance, a clear Christian contribution to this subject which is radically different from secular morality. Hence, people are attracted, rightly, to the person of Jesus and the possibility of a stance on war that is radically different, so it is held, from the tired, compromised thinking of men of affairs.

It has to be admitted that at this point fundamental disagreements about the foundation and nature of Christian ethics are bound to arise. The position taken here is that all people, whatever their religious beliefs or lack of them, have a sense of right and wrong; that there is a morality common to humanity as such. And that, whatever the effects of 'the fall', it is still possible for human beings to discern that some things are right and others wrong. This approach can be subsumed under the general heading of 'natural law' thinking, an approach which was out of favour for many years but which has shown some signs of being rehabilitated in a modified form. The 'just war' tradition belongs within the overall sphere of natural law thinking. In other words, anyone concerned to think seriously about the morality of warfare would, whatever their religious presuppositions, see that these conditions apply. You do not have to be a Christian to see that not anyone should be allowed to wage war, but only those to whom has been committed authority to defend their country. You do not have to be a Christian to see that war should be waged not for any cause but only one that is just; that war should be waged only as a very last resort and not for any pretext. The fact that these conditions can be seen to apply by anyone of good will is not detrimental to the Christian faith. First, for the most part, it has been Christian theologians who have developed them. Secondly, the whole thrust of the 'just war' tradition is to bring the sphere of war into the sphere of morality and to curtail the occasions on which war can be waged and to limit the damage which it inflicts. This is not distinctively Christian but it is certainly a concern that Christians, along with others, should be engaged in. Thirdly, there is an emphasis not only on public morality but on the morality of the individual and his or her motivation. War is to be waged with the right intention, not for aggrandizement or even honour but for a just peace. The whole thrust and spirit of the 'just war' tradition, whilst not exclusively Christian, is properly Christian.

George Bell, Bishop of Chichester, a speech to the House of Lords, 9 February 1944

I turn to the situation in February 1944, and the terrific devastation by Bomber Command of German towns. I do not forget the Luftwaffe, or its tremendous bombing of Belgrade, Warsaw, Rotterdam, London, Portsmouth, Coventry, Canterbury and many other places of military, industrial and cultural importance. Hitler is a barbarian. There is no decent person on the Allied side who is likely to suggest that we should make him our pattern or attempt to be competitors in that market. It is clear enough that large-scale bombing of enemy towns was begun by the

Nazis. I am not arguing that point at all. The question with which I am concerned is this. Do the Government understand the full force of what area bombardment is doing and is destroying now? Are they alive not only to the vastness of the material damage, much of which is irreparable, but also to the harvests they are laying up for the future relationships of the peoples of Europe as well as to its moral implications? The aim of the Allied bombing from the air, said the Secretary of State for Air at Plymouth on 22 January, is to paralyse German war industry and transport. I recognise the legitimacy of concentrated attacks on industrial and military objectives, on airfields and air bases, in view especially of the coming Second Front. I fully realise that in attacks on centres of war industry and transport the killing of civilians when it is the result of bona-fide military action is inevitable. But there must be a fair balance between the means employed and the purpose achieved. To obliterate a whole town because certain portions contain military and industrial establishments is to reject the balance.

Let me take two crucial instances, Hamburg and Berlin. Hamburg has a population of between one and two million people. It contains targets of immense military and industrial importance. It also happens to be the most democratic town in Germany where the anti-Nazi opposition was the strongest. Injuries to civilians resulting from bona-fide attacks on particular objectives are legitimate according to International Law. But owing to the methods used, the whole town is now a ruin. Unutterable destruction and devastation were wrought last autumn. On a very conservative estimate, according to the early German statistics, 28,000 people were killed. Never before in the history of air warfare was an attack of such weight and persistence carried out against a single industrial concentration. Practically all the buildings, cultural, military, residential, industrial, religious – including the famous University Library with its 800,000 volumes, of which three-quarters have perished – were razed to the ground.

Berlin, the capital of the Reich, is four times the size of Hamburg. The offices of the Government, the military, industrial war-making establishments in Berlin are a fair target. Injuries to civilians are inevitable. But up to date half Berlin has been destroyed, area by area, the residential and industrial proportions alike. Through the dropping of thousands of tons of bombs, including fire-phosphorus bombs, of extraordinary power, men and women have been lost, overwhelmed in the colossal tornado of smoke, blast and flame. It is said that 74,000 persons have been killed and that three million are already homeless. The policy is obliteration, openly acknowledged. This is not a justifiable act of war . . .

How is it then that this wholesale destruction has come about? The answer is that it is the method used, the method of area bombing. The first outstanding raid of area bombing was, I believe, in the spring of 1942, directed against Lübeck, then against Rostock, followed by the thousand-bomber raid against Cologne at the end of May 1942. The point I want to bring home, because I doubt whether it is sufficiently realised, that it is no longer definite military and industrial objectives, which are the aims of the bombers, but the whole town, area by area, is plotted carefully out. This area is singled out and plastered on one night; that area is singled out and plastered on another night; a third, a fourth, a fifth area is singled out and plastered night after night, till, to use the language of the Chief of Bomber Command with regard to Berlin, the heart of Nazi Germany ceases to beat. How can there be discrimination in such matters when civilians, monuments, military objectives and industrial objectives all together form the target? How can the bombers aim at anything more than a great space when they see nothing and the bombing is blind? Is it a matter of wonder that anti-Nazis who long for help to overthrow Hitler are driven to despair? I have here a telegram which I have communicated to the Foreign Office, sent to me on 27 December last by a well-known anti-Nazi Christian leader who had to flee from Germany for his life long before the war. It was sent from Zurich, and puts what millions inside Germany must feel: 'Is it understood that the present situation gives us no sincere opportunity for appeal to people because one cannot but suspect effect of promising words on practically powerless population convinced by bombs and phosphor that their annihilation is resolved?'

If we wish to shorten the war, as we must, then let the Government speak a word of hope and encouragement both to the tortured millions of Europe and to those enemies of Hitler to whom in 1939 Mr Churchill referred as 'millions who stand aloof from the seething mass of criminality and corruption constituted by the Nazi Party machine'.

Why is there this blindness to the psychological side? Why is there this forgetfulness of the ideals by which our cause is inspired? How can the War Cabinet fail to see that this progressive devastation of cities is threatening the roots of civilisation? How can they be blind to the harvest of even fiercer warring, the desolation, even in this country, to which the present destruction will inevitably lead when members of the War Cabinet have long passed to rest? How can they fail to realise that this is not the way to curb military aggression and end war? This is an extraordinarily solemn moment. What we do in war – which, after all, lasts a comparatively short time – affects the whole character of peace, which covers a much longer period. The sufferings of Europe, brought about by the demonic cruelty of Hitler and his Nazis, hardly imaginable to those in this country who for the last five years have not been out of this island or had intimate associations with Hitler's victims, are not to be healed by the use of power only, power exclusive and unlimited. The Allies stand for something greater than power. The chief name inscribed on our banner is 'law'. It is of supreme importance that we who, with our Allies, are the liberators of Europe should so use power that it is always under the control of law. It is because the bombing of enemy towns – this area bombing – raises this issue of power unlimited and exclusive that such immense importance is bound to attach to the policy and action of His Majesty's Government.

3.2 Some principles

The Church and the Bomb: Nuclear Weapons and Christian Conscience, **London, Hodder & Stoughton, 1982, pp. 87–8, 90–1**

Why should non-combatants be spared? The prohibition is an application of the more general moral principle that it is wrong to kill innocent people. In this context an innocent person is one who is unarmed and is not involved in the fighting. Those who are directly involved in the fighting have to that extent forfeited their immunity from direct attack, because it would be impossible to protect one's own people without attacking the former. Enemy non-combatants, however, have not put themselves in that position. To attack them is unjust. To kill them is murder. Killers may be attacked, no one else may.

It needs to be stressed that non-combatant immunity does not imply that non-combatants can be protected against all the consequences of warlike activity. Villagers whose homes lie just behind the front lines cannot reasonably expect their lives to be unaffected by the conflict going on around them. What the principle rules out is action taken intentionally against non-combatants by armed force.

The history of war offers examples both of the blatant ignoring of non-combatant immunity, and of the continuing struggle to ensure that it is observed. It is perhaps an indirect tribute to the importance of moral conviction that in recent times the over-stepping of the line, e.g. by the bombing of civilian populations, has been accompanied, where such a step seemed useful for military reasons, by a tendency to argue that prior violation of the rule by the other side gave exemption from the need to observe it. It is also argued that modern war is a war between whole societies. The line between combatants and non-combatants is an unreal one when the whole adult population is conscripted either to fight or to work in the war economy. In democratic societies, moreover, the people identify with their government's actions, and are encouraged to see the people of the nation with which they are at war as their own enemies.

In considering this argument a distinction needs to be drawn between the changes which have actually occurred in warfare in recent times, and the moral implications we wish to draw from them. While it is undoubtedly true that a modern civilian population feels implicated in the war effort to an extent that would have been unthinkable, say, two centuries ago, this does not necessarily affect what they actually do. Even in the last war, the majority of British civilians went on doing what they had been doing before the war started.

Undoubtedly there are borderline cases. Defence scientists, for example, and munition workers may do more harm to the enemy than many servicemen. But most people are not of this sort. This is most clearly seen if one considers women and children, the retired and the old. While they may in varying degrees support the war, they cannot be described as engaged in it. The fact that there are doubtful cases must not be allowed to paralyse judgement. Most cases are not doubtful.

. . .

Military activities which are directed at legitimate targets frequently kill or wound non-combatants, or harm their possessions. If such activities were to be judged immoral for that reason, it would hardly be possible to fight war at all. Moralists sometimes have recourse to the principle of double effect to determine whether such actions can be morally acceptable. (The phrase 'double effect' is needlessly obscure. It really refers to side effects.) This principle is not invoked in order to justify harming non-combatants, but rather to offer a conscientious serviceman, who is contemplating an action which he foresees may incidentally occasion such harm, a method of analysis to enable him to decide whether he is entitled to go ahead with the action.

The principle was developed by Roman Catholic theologians to handle cases in which a desired good end could only be pursued if the agent were willing to cause 'collateral' harm of a type which he would not be entitled to will as an end, or as a means to a good end. For example, a doctor cannot employ treatments such as chemotherapy for cancer without causing some unwanted side effects. These are not intended in the strict sense of the word, though it may be foreseen that they will probably, or even inevitably, follow. In that sense they are not intended by the doctor and can be described as incidental or accidental. Indeed, it would be a very strange doctor who intended them in the sense of setting his will on obtaining them, rather than regretting them and seeking to avoid and mitigate them.

The principle can be briefly stated: 'One is justified in permitting incidental evil effects from one's good actions if there is a proportionate reason.' It is presumed that if there were any less harmful way of achieving the desired good one would take it.

G. E. M. Anscombe, 'War and Murder', in Walter Stein (ed.), *Nuclear Weapons and Christian Conscience*, London, The Merlin Press, 1961, pp. 57–9

The distinction between the intended, and the merely foreseen, effects of a voluntary action is indeed absolutely essential to Christian ethics. For Christianity forbids a number of things as being bad in themselves. But if I am answerable for the foreseen consequences of an action or refusal, as much as for the action itself, then these prohibitions will break down. If someone innocent will die unless I do a wicked thing, then on this view I am his murderer in refusing: so all that is left to me is to weigh up evils. Here the theologian steps in with the principle of double effect and says: 'No, you are no murderer, if the man's death was neither your aim nor your chosen means, and if you had to act in the way that led to it or else do something absolutely forbidden'. Without understanding of this principle, anything can be – and is wont to be – justified, and the Christian teaching that in no circumstances may one commit murder, adultery, apostasy (to give a few examples) goes by the board. These absolute prohibitions of Christianity by no means exhaust its ethic; there is a large area where what is just is determined partly by a prudent weighing up of consequences. But the prohibitions are bedrock, and without them the Christian ethic goes to pieces. Hence the necessity of the notion of double effect.

At the same time, the principle has been repeatedly abused from the seventeenth century up till now. The causes lie in the history of philosophy. From the seventeenth century till now what may be called Cartesian psychology has dominated the thought of philosophers and theologians. According to this psychology, an intention was an interior act of the mind which could be produced at will. Now if intention is all important – as it is – in determining the goodness or badness of an action, then, on this theory of what intention is, a marvellous way offered itself of making any action lawful. You only had to 'direct your intention' in a suitable way. In practice, this means making a little speech to yourself: 'What I mean to be doing is . . .'

This perverse doctrine has occasioned repeated condemnations by the Holy See from the seventeenth century to the present day.

. . .

I know a Catholic boy who was puzzled at being told by his school-master that it was an *accident* that the people of Hiroshima and Nagasaki were there to be killed; in fact, however absurd it seems, such thoughts are common among priests who know that they are forbidden by the divine law to justify the direct killing of the innocent.

It is nonsense to pretend that you do not intend to do what is the means you take to your chosen end. Otherwise there is absolutely no substance to the Pauline teaching that we may not do evil that good may come.

3.3 Nuclear war and nuclear deterrence

Anthony Kenny, 'Postscript: Counterforce and Countervalue', in Walter Stein (ed.), *Nuclear Weapons and Christian Conscience,* **London, The Merlin Press, 1961, pp. 160–2 (Postscript © 1963)**

On 16 June, 1962, Mr. Robert McNamara, the American Defense Secretary, made a speech in which he denounced independent national nuclear deterrents as 'dangerous, expensive, prone to obsolescence, and lacking in credibility as a deterrent'. Surprise nuclear attack, he said, was not a rational act; but nations did not always act rationally. The NATO allies must frame their strategy with the terrible contingency of nuclear war in mind (*The Observer*, 17.6.62).

In the course of the same speech, however, Mr. McNamara announced that in the event of a major war American strategy would be aimed at the destruction of enemy military forces, not of the civilian population. This, he said, would 'give a possible opponent the strongest imaginable incentive to refrain from striking our own cities'.

The American Secretary of Defense thus gave official sanction to a distinction drawn by nuclear strategists between a 'counterforce strategy' aimed at knocking out the enemy's strategic forces, and a 'countervalue strategy' aimed at destroying his cities. Since this distinction resembles the distinction made by Catholic teaching between the lawful and unlawful use of bombs in war, it is worth looking more closely at Mr. McNamara's strategy to see whether, unlike the policy of President Eisenhower, it is capable of moral justification.

On examination it appears that Mr. McNamara by no means ruled out the eventual application of countervalue strategy. In the same speech he spoke of America's 'second-strike capability' as a deterrent to enemy attack on American cities. It appears therefore that the restriction of American aim to military targets in the event of war would be only a temporary measure. The strength and nature of the NATO alliance, *The Times* reported him as saying, 'made it possible for the United States to retain, even in the face of a massive attack, sufficient reserve power to destroy an enemy society if driven to it' (*The Times*, 18.6.62). Thus the old threat remained, relegated only to second place.

Some days later the American Defense Department issued estimates of casualties likely to be caused in the West if both the Soviet Union and the United States adopted a counterforce strategy in the event of a nuclear war. The estimates were given in *The Times* as follows:

> According to these official estimates the casualties in the West would be 25 million dead, compared with 215 million if cities were bombarded. The estimates are divided as follows: In the event of a counterforce exchange, 10 million dead in the United States and 15 million in Western Europe, including Britain; in a general bombardment, 100 million in the United States and 115 million in Western Europe.

Other American experts put the figures much higher. Herman Kahn, for instance, estimated that Western casualties might reach 125 million (*The Times*, 4.7.62). Such figures shed a lurid light on what Mr. McNamara meant by 'aiming at the destruction of military forces'. To claim that a counterforce strategy of this kind does not involve an attack on civilian populations is like claiming not to be responsible for the death of a friend if one shoots a bullet to kill a mosquito perched on his throat.

Richard Harries, 'The Morality of Nuclear Deterrence', in Richard Harries (ed.), *What Hope in an Armed World?*, Basingstoke, Pickering & Inglis, 1982, pp. 100–2, 105–6

If it is true that deterrence and its failure are fundamentally different situations it is misleading to apply the morality of the use of weapons in a wooden way to the morality of possession and threatened use. If a terrorist threatens to blow up a school full of children and by chance I have access to the family of the terrorist, and the only way I can stop him from carrying out his threat is by telling him that if he does I will inflict comparable damage on his children, then terrible though it may be, I may have to make that threat. It is the only hold I have over the terrorist, the only way I can try to save the children. But if the terrorist carried out his threat and did blow up the school, then there would be a completely different situation. Actually hurting the terrorist's children could not possibly be justified. It would simply be an act of revenge.

Nevertheless, for deterrence to work the enemy must believe that in certain circumstances we would actually carry out our threat. And as has already been said, not every use of nuclear weapons must be regarded as intrinsically immoral. The use of low yield weapons on relatively isolated military targets might be morally legitimate. And although the use of nuclear weapons on military targets near centres of population would be in danger of being disproportionate, must the deterrent effect provided by the thought of that damage be condemned in the same way? The American moral theologian Paul Ramsey, thinks not. He writes of 'a direct and wanted effect of the unwanted, indirect, collateral consequences of even just use of nuclear weapons'. Then, of course, the very possession of nuclear weapons is a deterrent, irrespective of whether threats are made about possible targets. There will always be uncertainty in the mind of an enemy that the weapons might be used. However, this is to soft-peddle the issue, which is, does deterrence depend on *threatening to do what is immoral*? Does deterrence in the end rest on making a credible threat that *in extremis* nuclear weapons will be used at or near enemy cities? McGeorge Bundy has recently stressed that mutual assured destruction is a basic condition, not one doctrine among many, for the nuclear age. It has to be agreed that this is so. For those who stand in the Just War tradition the threat that nuclear weapons might be used directly against cities is a threat to contravene the principle of non-combatant immunity. Group Captain Leonard Cheshire told me once that he had been in correspondence with Caspar Weinberger about the possibility of NATO making a declaration that they would not use nuclear weapons against cities. This would not completely undermine deterrence because even if such a declaration were made there would still be uncertainty in an enemy's mind that we might attack cities. However it is difficult to see any government making such a statement, for the threat that we might in certain extreme circumstances aim nuclear weapons at enemy cities is a keystone in the arch of deterrence. It is a final threat to be kept in case all else fails: a threat, terrible as it is, that increases the caution of potential adversaries.

Is such a threat to be regarded as bluff? No, for there are not only threats but people trained to carry out those threats. As Walter Stein put it, 'a multi-billion pound industry and an enormous apparatus of threats and threateners, of chains of command into which all these agents are locked, and of step-by-step emergency reflexes, to substantiate these threats, reduces the "bluff" excuse to total intellectual and moral non-sense.' But is it immoral to threaten to do what it would be immoral to actually do? Dr Barrie Paskins argues that it is. He too dismisses the 'bluff' defence, for much the same reasons as Stein, and then considers various arguments that have been put forward to save the threat to use nuclear weapons from the moral condemnation that using them would bring forth. But he is not convinced. 'I conclude that the Soviet and Western deterrents are rightly characterised in terms of the conditional intention to wage, *in extremis*, all-out nuclear war; and that they as well as all-out nuclear war are immoral.'

. . .

How is it that people with reasonably sensitive consciences are able to live with this moral dilemma? It is that nuclear deterrence is a necessity, whatever Just War theorising says about it, because to give it up would leave a nation helpless against antagonistic nuclear powers, and to do that would be even more immoral. The concept of necessity is a danger-ous one; it is also ambiguous. It can either mean that states always and inevitably take whatever steps are necessary and within their power to protect their vital interests, or that they ought to take such steps. I use the word to indicate the idea that they *ought* to take such steps. This is a highly dangerous idea for it allows an unscrupulous statesman to justify anything in the name of necessity. Nevertheless, however much we might condemn statesmen in past ages for misusing the idea, it is one that cannot be avoided; and it is not unknown to moralists. Jeremy Taylor wrote in the seventeenth century, 'he that is injured may drive away the injury, he may fight against invaders, he may divert the war if necessary; but he may not destroy the innocent with the guilty, the peaceable coun-trymen with the fighting soldiers: and nothing can legitimate that but an absolute necessity.' If we ask, 'an absolute necessity for what?', the answer is the survival of the state.

But this rightly draws forth the further question; why should the state be given this pre-eminent value? It is possible for cultural and moral values to survive without an independent state. Jewish values survived, despite terrible persecution, without a state of their own. The Chinese, though often conquered, have tended to assimilate their conquerors rather than be assimilated themselves. Could not the same apply if Western societies had to surrender to an enemy with an alien ideology? But Western societies 'are what they are largely by virtue of the close interlocking of a system of material organisation and power with a body of ideals and principles . . . Destroy the organisation and the power and you destroy the effective operation of the ideals and principles.' In other words, what is of value in democracy and in the whole range of democratic rights, cannot exist in a vacuum. It is enshrined in and expressed through particular societies and political systems. Therefore in a world where states have different perceptions and conflicting interests, in a world where the causes of war are still with us, and where some powers have nuclear weapons, it is not possible for a major power to have even tolerable security without possessing nuclear weapons. Nuclear deterrence comes under the head of 'absolute necessity'.

Peacemaking in a Nuclear Age: A Report of a Working Party of the Board for Social Responsibility of the General Synod of the Church of England, London, Church House Publishing, 1988, pp. 49–50

Clements remarks . . . that 'There can be no nuclear patriotism'; and if the account of patriotism developed in these pages is correct then the linking of nuclear hawkishness to patriotic seriousness is a mistake. It is possible to be patriotic, to be committed to one's place and people, without imagining that this must involve the quest for a total and exclusive security based on a massive and expanding nuclear arsenal. For the Christian, indeed, this is the only possibility, since the Christian above all is bound to search for a security that can be shared, and that rests on something more durably humane than total and permanent threat. There are some who argue that the maintenance of a minimum deterrent, combined with the active pursuit of arms reductions, is an unhappy necessity for the foreseeable future; but such people will recognise the danger in tying armaments to national pride and to the fantasy quest for final invulnerability. There are others who will argue that the mere possession of a nuclear arsenal entails the wrong kind of loyalty to country. But on both sides of this divide there can be agreement that there is a Christian case for commitment to and defence of the state in certain conditions, *and* an agreement about the dangers of mindless and uncritical loyalty, especially to a state whose obsession with security gradually destroys what it seeks to defend, and reproduces the very tyranny it fears. The common ground on which such Christian commentators may meet is, finally, that of the shared loyalty implicit in a shared baptism, being pledged to the vision of the Kingdom and to the God who has shown himself loyal to the world. This is never, though, loyalty to a purely abstract or ideal humanity; it is learned in the particular communities we cannot help belonging to, communities rightly loved, but loved for the sake of a greater community.

Jean Bethke Elshtain, *Women and War*, New York, Basic Books, 1987, p. 258

For the political embodiment of the attitude I here suggest, I return to the chastened patriot. He or she has no illusions: recognizing the limiting conditions internal to international politics, this civic being does not embrace utopian fantasies of world government or total disarmament. For neither the arms-control option (as currently defined) nor calls for immediate disarmament are bold: the first, because it is a way of doing business as usual; the second, because it covertly sustains business as usual by proclaiming solutions that lie outside the reach of possibility.

Devirilizing discourse, in favor not of feminization (for the feminized and masculinized emerged in tandem and both embody dangerous distortions) but of politicization, the chastened patriot constitutes men and women as citizens who share what Hannah Arendt calls 'the faculty of action.' This citizen is skeptical about the forms and claims of the sovereign state; recognizes the (phony) parity in the notion of *equally* 'sovereign states,' and is thereby alert to the many forms hegemony can take; and deflates fantasies of control. Taking a cue from Arendt, this citizen gives 'forgiveness' a central role as one way human beings have to break cycles of vengeance. *Ascesis* – a refraining or withholding, a refusal to bring all one's force to bear – surfaces, in this vision of things, as a strength not a weakness.

As Americans, citizens of . . . a strong and dominant nation of awesome potential force, we are invited to take unilateral initiatives in order to break symbolically the cycle of vengeance and fear signified by that very force. As individual men and women we are invited to examine, and take up, the alternatives, woven throughout the story of women and war, to identities that lock us inside the traditional, and dangerous, narrative of war and peace.

3.4 Judgement and revelation

Andrew Chester, 'The Apocalypse and the Nuclear Holocaust', in *In God We Trust: Christian Reflections on the Nuclear Arms Race*, London, CND Publications, 1986, pp. 59–62

In recent years much confusion has been caused among Christians by the misuse of parts of the apocalyptic writings of the Bible – that is, Daniel, and above all, the book of Revelation. Indeed, the whole book of Revelation is popularly understood as consisting simply of crude predictions of the final destruction of the world, and a world-weariness born of complete despair with the course of events at the time it was written. Hence, it is on Revelation especially that attention is concentrated here. Words and images from it have been used quite casually in relation to the end of the world and nuclear war. Thus 'Armageddon' (Revelation 16:16) has become a kind of umbrella word to depict the nuclear holocaust. Similarly, the word 'apocalyptic' itself is commonly used of this threat, apparently in the sense of something which is final, imminent and inevitable.

What I find even more alarming is that the book of Revelation has been enthusiastically used, from an apparently Christian perspective, in support of the possession and potential use of nuclear weapons. Not so long ago, President Reagan spoke rather ominously of his excitement at seeing things work out in an apocalyptic sort of way. The general tenor of this statement appears all too close to a recent line of biblical interpretation (associated especially with the Moral Majority movement in North America, and with fringe and pseudo-Christian sects) which holds that the nuclear holocaust is predicted in Revelation, and that God's purpose is now being brought to fulfilment.

. . .

We should be under no illusion about the potentially serious consequences of using Scripture in such a way. But it is precisely for this reason that we should not simply ignore Revelation, or wish that it wasn't in the New Testament at all. To do that would be to abandon it to this sort of abuse. On the contrary, we need to show how Revelation can have positive significance for our own situation.

. . .

[T]here is strong emphasis in Revelation on *divine judgement* and the consequences of *the lack of human repentance*. It is the failure to repent that brings down divine judgement and wrath . . . This is in fact a theme that permeates the whole work. It is anticipated in the letters to the seven churches in Chapters 2–3; thus, for example, in 2:21f it is said of the false prophetess Jezebel:

> I gave her time to repent, but she refuses to repent of her immorality. Behold, I will throw her on a sickbed, and those who commit adultery with her I will throw into great tribulation, unless they repent of her doings.

This is taken up in the vision of the great harlot in Chapter 17. Thus 17:1f:

Come, I will show you the judgement of the great harlot who is seated upon many waters, with whom the kings of the earth have committed fornication, and with the wine of whose fornication the dwellers on earth have become drunk.

The harlot, Babylon, (that is, imperial Rome), is set on the beast, the empire (verse 3), and appears all-powerful and glorious. But it has achieved its position through evil deeds and exploitation, and has exercised it with ruthless arrogance. Hence it has also brought about its own judgement and destruction. It is the beast itself that destroys the harlot (verses 16ff). Thus its power is illusory, its grandeur and supremacy ephemeral. Rome has denied God and exulted unrepentingly in its own strength and self-sufficiency. This is its downfall, and it is for this reason that God will make it perish at the hands of its own empire. Thus the city of Rome, in its reliance on earthly power and possessions and in its corruptness, stands in complete contrast to the heavenly city, the new Jerusalem, of Chapter 21, the pure and perfect 'bride' that belongs in heaven with God, and comes from there to 'man'. In short, Revelation points to the inevitability of the collapse of a society which denies God's righteousness (cf. also e.g. 9:20).

The main message of Revelation, then, is one of judgement and the need for repentance. It is therefore vital to appreciate, in the specific context of the nuclear debate, that it is not simply peace that we can be concerned with, if we take proper account of what Revelation tells us. What is involved here, from the perspective of Revelation, is judgement on society, a judgement indeed to which society cannot respond, precisely because of its own corruption. And a society which fails to respond has already sown the seeds of its own destruction. Therefore this Christian discipleship involves the unpleasant task of invoking God's judgement on a society that denies God and refuses to repent. But that judgement is properly invoked on a society which arrogantly asserts its self-sufficiency and security on the basis of an ever-increasing and more sophisticated nuclear arsenal, while simultaneously denying God's righteousness and fundamental justice for the weakest in its own society and, still worse, those in developing countries who lack the basic essentials of life itself.

Topics for discussion

1 In what sense may just war theory be called Christian? Upon what, if any, Christian principles, is it founded?
2 Who are the innocent in war? Assess the attempts of just war theory to determine the conditions under which civilian deaths may be foreseen as a legitimate, if regretted, consequence of one's actions.
3 Does just war theory rule out the moral legitimacy of waging a nuclear war? Is there any other way in which a Christian might justify fighting a nuclear war? Is the notion of 'necessity' or 'compromise' of any relevance?
4 Is a policy of nuclear deterrence morally justifiable?
5 Can a Christian be a patriot? Or do higher commitments destroy any legitimacy in the use of the term?
6 How may the Bible be used, if at all, in discussions of modern warfare?
7 'We call upon the churches to give up any theological and moral justification of the use of military power, be it in war or through other forms of oppressive security systems, and to become public advocates of a just peace' (Konrad Raiser, Evangelical Lutheran Church, Germany, 1991). Does the advocacy of a just peace require the repudiation of just war theory?

4 Holy wars and holy tolerance

4.1 *Jihad* in Islam

Sachiko Murata and William C. Chittick, *The Vision of Islam: The Foundations of Muslim Faith and Practice,* **London, I. B. Tauris, 1996, pp. 20–2**

Some authorities have held that there is a sixth pillar of Islam: jihad. This word has become well-known in English because of the contemporary political situation and the focus of the media on violence. Hence, a bit more attention has been paid to it than would be warranted if we were simply looking at the role jihad plays in Islam.

The first thing one needs to understand about the term *jihad* is that 'holy war' is a highly misleading and usually inaccurate translation. In Islamic history, the label has been applied to any war by 'our side'. Until very recently in the West, the situation was similar; every war was considered holy, because God was on our side. By employing the term, Muslims condemned the other side as anti-God. In short, the word has played the role of patriotic slogans everywhere. To undertake a jihad is, in contemporary terms, 'to fight for the preservation of democracy and freedom'. It is to do what the good people do.

The Koranic usage of the term *jihad* is far broader than the political use of the term might imply. The basic meaning of the term is 'struggle'. Most commonly, the Koran uses the verb along with the expression 'in the path of God'. The 'path of God' is of course the path for right conduct that God has set down in the Koran and the example of the Prophet.

From one point of view, jihad is simply the complement to *islam*. The word *islam*, after all, means 'submission' or 'surrender'. Westerners tend to think of this as a kind of passivity. But surrender takes place to God's will, and it is God's will that people struggle in His path. Hence submission demands struggle. Receptivity toward God's command requires people to be active toward all the negative tendencies in society and themselves that pull them away from God. In this perspective, submission to God and struggle in his path go together harmoniously, and neither is complete without the other.

Within the Islamic context, the fact that submission to God demands struggle in his path is self-evident. *Salat*, *zakat*, fasting, and hajj are all struggle. If you think they are easy, try performing the *salat* according to the rules for a few days. In fact, the biggest obstacles people face in submitting themselves to God are their own laziness and lack of imagination. People let the currents of contemporary opinion and events carry them along without resisting. It takes an enormous struggle to submit to an authority that breaks not only with one's own likes and dislikes, but also with the pressure of society to conform to the crowd.

The place of jihad in the divine plan is typically illustrated by citing words that the Prophet uttered on one occasion when he had returned to Medina from a battle with the enemies of the new religion. He said, 'We have returned from the lesser jihad to the greater jihad.' The people said, 'O Messenger of God, what jihad could be greater than struggling against the unbelievers with the sword?' He replied, 'Struggling against the enemy in your own breast.'

In later texts, this inward struggle is most often called *mujahada* rather than jihad. Grammatically, the word *mujahada* – which is derived from the same root as jihad – means exactly the same thing. But the word *jihad* came to be employed to refer to outward wars as well as the inward struggle against one's own negative tendencies, while the word *mujahada* is used almost exclusively for the greater, inward jihad.

Those Muslim scholars who have said that jihad is the sixth pillar of Islam have usually had in mind the fact that struggle in the path of God is a necessity for all Muslims. At the same time, they recognize that this struggle will sometimes take the outward form of war against the enemies of Islam.

But it needs to be stressed that in the common language of Islamic countries, the word *jihad* is used for any war. In a similar way, most Americans have considered any war engaged in by the United States as a just war. But from the point of view of the strict application of Islamic teachings, most so-called jihads have not deserved the name. Any king (or dictator, as we have witnessed more recently) can declare a jihad. There were always a few of the religious authorities who would lend support to the king – such as the scholar whom the king had appointed to be chief preacher at the royal mosque. But there have usually been a good body of ulama who have not supported wars simply because kings declared them. Rather, they would only support those that followed the strict application of Islamic teachings. By these standards, it is probably safe to say that there have been few if any valid jihads in the past century, and perhaps not for the past several hundred years

4.2 The Qur'anic texts

These texts from the Qur'an are taken from two sources:

Arthur J. Arberry, *The Koran Interpreted*, Oxford, Oxford University Press, 1983

N. J. Dawood, *The Koran: With Parallel Arabic Text*, London, Penguin, 1994

(1)
'And fight in the way of God with those who fight with you, but aggress not; God loves not the aggressors. And slay them wherever you come upon them and expel them from where they expelled you; persecution is more grievous than slaying. But fight them not by the Holy Mosque until they should fight you there: then, if they fight you, slay them – such is the recompense of unbelievers – but if they give over, surely God is All-forgiving, All-compassionate.' (2:187–8; Arberry, p. 25)

(2)
'So do thou fight in the way of God; thou art charged only with thyself. And urge on the unbelievers; haply God will restrain the unbelievers' might; God is stronger in might, more terrible in punishing.' (4:86; Arberry, p. 84)

(3)
A proclamation to the people from God and His apostle on the day of the greater pilgrimage:

God and His apostle are under no obligation to the idolaters. If you repent, it shall be well with you; but if you give no heed, know that you shall not be immune from God's judgement.

Proclaim a woeful punishment to the unbelievers, except to those idolaters who have honoured their treaties with you in every detail and aided none against you. With these keep faith, until their treaties have run their term. God loves the righteous.

. . .

Believers, why is it that when you are told: 'March in the cause of God,' you linger slothfully in the land? Are you content with this life in preference to the life to come? Few indeed are the blessings of this life, compared to those of the life to come.

If you do not go to war, He will punish you sternly, and replace you by other men. You will in no way harm Him: for God has power over all things.

If you do not help him, God will help him as He helped him when he was driven out by the unbelievers with one other. In the cave he said to his companion: 'Do not despair, God is with us.' God caused His tranquillity to descend upon him and sent to his aid invisible warriors, so that he routed the unbelievers and exalted the Word of God. God is mighty and wise.

Whether unarmed or well-equipped, march on and fight for the cause of God, with your wealth and with your persons. This will be best for you, if you but knew it.

. . .

It shall be no offence for the disabled, the sick, and those lacking the means to stay behind: if they are true to God and His apostle. The righteous shall not be blamed: God is forgiving and merciful. Nor shall those be blamed who, when they came to you demanding conveyances to the battle-front and you could find none to carry them, went away in tears grieving that they had not the means to contribute.

The offenders are those that seek exemption although they are men of wealth. They are content to be with those who stay behind. God has set a seal upon their hearts; they are devoid of knowledge.

When you return they will come up to you with excuses. Say: 'Make no excuses: we will not believe you. God has revealed to us the truth about you. God and His apostle will watch your actions. Then you shall return to Him who knows alike the unknown and the manifest, and He will declare to you what you have done.'

When you return they will appeal to you in God's name to let them be. So let them be: they are unclean. Hell shall be their home, the punishment for their misdeeds.

. . .

God has purchased from the faithful their lives and worldly goods and in return has promised them the Garden. They will fight for the cause of God, slay and be slain. Such is the true promise which He has made them in the Torah, the Gospel and the Koran. And who is more true to his pledge than God? Rejoice then in the bargain you have made. That is the supreme triumph.

Those that repent and those that serve and praise Him; those that fast and those that kneel and prostrate themselves; those that enjoin justice, forbid evil, and observe the commandments of God, shall be richly rewarded. Proclaim the good tidings to the faithful.

It is not for the Prophet or the believers to beg forgiveness for idolaters, even though they be related to them, after it has become manifest that they have earned the punishment of Hell. Abraham prayed for his father only to fulfil a promise he had made him. But when he realized he was an enemy of God, he disowned him. Yet Abraham was a compassionate and tender-hearted man. (9:3–4, 38–41, 91–5, 111–14; Dawood, pp. 186, 192–3, 200–1, 203–4)

(4)
'. . . bow you down and prostrate yourselves, and serve your Lord, and do good; haply so you shall prosper; and struggle for God as is His due, for He has chosen you, and has laid on you no impediment in your religion, being the creed of your father Abraham.' (22:76–7; Arberry, p. 342)

(5)
'So obey not the unbelievers, but struggle with them thereby mightily.' (25:54; Arberry, p. 366)

(6)
'But those who struggle in Our (i.e. God's) cause, surely We shall guide them in Our ways; and God is with those who do good.' (26:69; Arberry, p. 410)

(7)
'You shall believe in God and His Messenger, and struggle in the way of God with your possessions and yourselves.' (61:11; Arberry, p. 581)

4.3 Muslim–Christian relations

Bernard Lewis, 'Politics and War', in Joseph Schacht with C. E. Bosworth (eds), *The Legacy of Islam*, Oxford, Oxford University Press, 1974, pp. 180–1

The clash between Islam and Christendom began during the lifetime of the Prophet. In the earlier stages of his career, when the main fight was against Arab paganism, his attitude to the Jews and the Christians was friendly and respectful. The leadership of the community brought him into contact and then conflict with both. At first the Jews, strongly represented at Medina, were the immediate enemy, while the Christians remained potential allies and converts. Later, when the expanding influence of the community of Medina brought the Muslims into collision with Christian tribes in Arabia and on the northern borders, relations with Christianity, as with Judaism, culminated in war:

> Fight against those who do not believe in Allah nor in the Last Day, who do not forbid what Allah and His Apostle have forbidden, nor practise the true religion, among those who have been given the Book, until they pay the *jizya* from their hand, they being humbled. The Jews say: "Uzayr is the son of God.' The Christians say 'Christ is the son of God.' This is what they say, with their own mouths, imitating what was said by the unbelievers before. May God fight them! How they are deceived! (Koran, 9:29–30)

[*The term jizya was later specialized to mean the poll-tax paid by the non-Muslim subjects of the Muslim state. In the Koran it probably has the more general meaning of payment or recompense. The Muslim tradition identifies 'Uzayr with the Biblical Ezra. The significance of this phrase has baffled modern scholarship.*]

These verses were taken as abrogating previous revelations which expressed a friendlier and more hopeful attitude to the non-Muslims; they provided the scriptural basis for the legal doctrines which required Muslims to fight and conquer the Christians and Jews, and, if they refused Islam, to impose on them fiscal and social penalties.

W. Montgomery Watt, *Islamic Political Thought: The Basic Concepts,* Edinburgh, Edinburgh University Press, 1968, pp. 48–9, 51

Even after most of the fighting came to be done by professionals, these had always to be Muslims. In times of special emergency other Muslims might be asked to volunteer for military service. There was no question of any non-Muslim, a member of the 'protected minorities' (to be described presently), taking part in the military expeditions of an Islamic state. This tradition has never been abandoned, at least not until very recent times. In the Ottoman empire military service continued to be only for Muslims. In the middle of the nineteenth century the 'protected minorities' were filled with dismay when it was suggested that they should share a common Ottoman nationality with the Muslims, since this would have meant liability for military service.

Perhaps this reluctance to allow non-Muslims to fight was linked with the fact that most of the wars in which an Islamic army would fight would be 'holy wars', fought 'in the way of God'. Sir John Bagot Glubb (Glubb Pasha), speaking from long experience of military affairs in the Arab world, finds that there reappears in recent Arab revolutions 'the old idea that the army is the guardian of the nation's morals'. Thus is the contemporary Islamic world linked with its roots in the past.

The relation of the Muslims to the Jews and the Christians had been a problem from the time of the Hijra [*the departure of Muhammad from Mecca to Medina in 622*]. The Qur'an speaks of the revelation to Muhammad as repeating and confirming previous revelations, especially the Torah of the Jews (or Old Testament) and the Injil ('evangel') or New Testament of the Christians. Muhammad consequently expected Jews and Christians to accept him as the Messenger of God. It soon became clear that the Jews of Medina were not prepared to do this. As for the Christians, there were so few contacts during Muhammad's early years at Medina that he may still have hoped they would accept him. The Jews of Medina apparently had a treaty relationship with Muhammad from the beginning. When it came to hostilities with Jews outside Medina – those at Khaybar – they were accepted, on their defeat and surrender, into the Pax Islamica, but as a payment for this protection they had to pay to the Muslims a proportion of their date harvest. There are also reports of treaties with the Christians of Ayla (biblical Elath, modern Akaba), the Jews of Maqna near by, and other small groups encountered during the expedition to Tabuk in 630. In general these small groups were said to receive 'the protection (*jiwar, dhimma*) of God and of his Messenger';

they retained their internal structure of government; and in return they made a payment, usually in kind.

. . .

One of the reasons why the system worked well was that among the pre-Islamic Arabs it had been a matter of honour for the desert tribe to show that its protection was effective, and something of this attitude to the *dhimmis* passed to Muslim rulers. On the whole there was more genuine toleration of non-Muslims under Islam than there was of non-Christians in medieval Christian states. There were exceptions, of course. When times were hard and difficult, non-Muslims would tend to get the worst of it. Occasionally, too, a ruler, in order to divert animosity from himself, would encourage the mob to vent its feelings on the *dhimmis*. On the whole, however, the 'protected minorities' had a tolerable existence.

4.4 Islam and peace

Sayid Mujtaba and Rukni Musawa Lari, *Western Civilisation Through Muslim Eyes,* **ET Huston, Texas, Free Islamic Literatures, 1979, pp. 130–4**

When freedom of thought and of choice of the best way of life is taken from men, force, either of police or of army, must be called in. It was to reduce oppressors and tyrants to subjection, in order that the oppressed might be freed to listen to the challenge of Islam, that the first Muslim battles took place. The masses must be given freedom to make their own choice; for without that the truth cannot come to control societies, nations and the world. As it is written in Sura IV: Nisa'a – 'Women' (verse 75): 'Why should you not take up the Jehad in God's cause, and for the cause of the weak in Mecca, your own men, women and children, who cry out: "Our Lord! rescue us from this town of oppressors; and raise up for us a protector, and appoint for us a helper"?'

Islam does not war against people. It wars against oppression, tyranny and wrong. These false ideas it seeks to root out, and to replace them by the superior ideas of purity and faith. It seeks not to win over enemies, but to win enemies over to its – that is God's – side, in the eternal battle between good and evil. For humanity faces the choice between self-annihilation through evil on the one hand or the kingdom of God on earth through obedience on the other. There is no third way. To serve or to seek anything other than God and His will is idolatry. The worship of possessions, self, or power is as much idolatry as sacrificing to stock and stone. It is a negation of man's true nature and destiny.

. . .

In his book entitled 'War and Peace in Islam', Dr Majid Khadouri writes on page 214:

> Islam changed the old Arab conception of the 'Dar-ul-Harb' or House of War into that of the 'Dar-ul-Islam' or House of Islam, which truly sought to minister Islam to the people of the world. Its first success was in uniting the nations which accepted it within themselves, so that civil wars ceased. It went on to found a family of Islamic nations at peace with each other. It aims to bring that blessing to the whole world. Thus the aim of the Jehad is peace on earth, and that will be its final result.

Western Crusaders developed their concept of chivalry from the conduct of the Muslim paladins in war. One great principle was that the lives of the many poorer folk should be saved by settling the issue of the dispute in a single combat between two champions each chosen to represent his own side.

A whole range of courteous attitudes and actions was developed to govern such contests. They were carried over into the peaceful contests called 'jousts', in which knights fought each other to show their prowess before their monarch and their people, and also to practice against the day when they would be meeting the champion of an opposing army in serious warfare. The chivalrous and knightly conduct towards the fallen foe, which these contests taught, altered the entire manners of renascent Europe as it emerged from the barbarism of its latest invaders from the North. Ransoms were exacted and paid with honour.

Muslim armies were forbidden to cause the destruction of property, the burning of houses, the wasting of crops and pastures, the filling of wells or the deprivation of food. Mercy must be shown to the conquered. The utmost consideration must be manifested towards the enemy's children, aged, women and sick, whether mentally or physically afflicted.

. . .

The Prophet, sending his troops to fight, is reported by the book on the Jehad (Volume 2, p. 424) to have addressed them in the following terms:

Go in God's name for God's cause with God's aid, and act as God wishes you to act. Show no treachery or falsehood towards His commands. Mutilate no one. Show mercy to the aged, the incapable, women and children. Only when it is inevitable cut down a tree. Grant sanctuary to any prisoner from the least to the highest in order that they may hear the word of truth. Whoso follows that truth becomes your brother. If he refuses, release him to go to his home when peace is made. At all times and in every situation pray for God's help and obey His guidance about your conduct.

. . .

We were all brought up on the story of the Imam Ali laying an opponent prone and sitting on his chest to reason with him about the true faith: whereat the foeman spat in the saint's face. Ali at once rose and walked away. His followers asked him why, and he said:

I felt rage rising in my heart at that man's insult, and was tempted to slay him on the spot. If I had done so, it would not have been a just execution of a recalcitrant infidel because of his invincible ignorance, but an act of personal revenge under the impulse of passion. What is the good of my seeking to reason with him and bring him to a true faith unless I am living that true faith with a pure heart and free from pollution myself?

In the Holy Qur'an such an attitude is enjoined in many places, for instance in Sura II: Baqara – 'The Heifer' (verse 194): 'If anyone transgresses against you requite him with an exactly like action and restrain yourself for God; and know that God is with those who so restrain themselves.'

. . .

Nor did the Muslims force peoples of occupied lands to change their religion.

Islam arranged a system by which they guaranteed freedom of religion to believers in any of the heavenly books by forming them into 'Millats', semi-autonomous communities within the state with the right to their own forms of worship, to their customs at birth, at marriage and at death, to their own schools and the use of their own tongue if they had a language of their own like Turkish, Armenian, Kurdish, or Aramaic. They were exempt from the 'Zakat' or 'Tax in aid of the poor' which was incumbent on all Muslims. This exemption was because the Zakat has a religious as well as a political side. Instead they paid a poll tax because they were not Muslims. Payment of the poll tax guaranteed their citizenship rights in the whole community. Thus Islam guarded the tenderest scruples of conscience of followers of the revealed religions. It extended this care in its lawgiving to the treatment of criminals, of civil causes, of commercial matters, as well as the strictly religious side of life, so that the minorities were free and safeguarded in the following of their convictions.

. . .

Christian and Jewish minorities live under exemplary conditions in Islamic countries, in a coexistence where each respects the other's rights. When the Prophet first came to Yathrib many Jewish groups lived there, and dwelt alongside the Muslims without the least friction, a condition which was continued by the Caliphs after the Prophet's death. The Founder of Islam said: 'Whosoever harms a tribute-paying infidel living amongst us has harmed me.' And again: 'Beware! whosoever injures a non-Muslim, or steals even a worn-out piece of cloth or takes the smallest thing he owns without his consent, will find me on the side of the prosecution when he comes to trial on the Day of Judgment.'

When the Imam Ali was Caliph he one day came across a blind and helpless old man and asked for information about him. His officials told him that the old man was a Christian who in his youth and strength had been a civil servant. The saint replied: 'You used him for work when he was young and cast him off when he is old and weak! He must be given a pension from the public treasury to ensure his livelihood.'

Dr Laura Vacceia Vaglieri writes that the words of the Prophet and the Fatvas (ex-cathedra decrees) of the great Islamic jurisconsults show up the falsehood of the story that Islam imposed its religion by the sword. The Qur'an lays down that 'compulsion has no place in religion.'

4.5 Arab and Jew

Y. Harkabi, *Arab Attitudes to Israel*, ET London, Vallentine, Mitchell, 1972, pp. 219–22

The truth is that this tolerance of Islam toward the Jews was founded on discrimination! it was a tolerance towards inferiors. Morroe Berger, in *The Arab World*, sums up the position: 'Tolerance was not equality' (p. 259). According to the basic Islamic approach, there was no room for pagans, who must be destroyed, but the Jewish and Christian 'People of the Scripture' were recognized as inferior groups. Professor Von Grunebaum says:

> Their personal safety and their personal property are guaranteed them at the price of permanent inequality. (*Medieval Islam*, p. 178)

. . .

He adds that non-Muslims, indeed, sometimes rose to high positions in the State, but this was illegal, and was opposed by religious circles.

Professor Bernard Lewis describes their position as follows:

> The Dhimmis were second-class citizens, paying a high rate of taxation, suffering from certain social disabilities, and on a few rare occasions subjected to open persecution. But by and large their position was infinitely superior to that of those communities who differed from the established church in Europe. (*The Arabs in History*, p. 94)

The position of the Jews in the Arab countries was not so idyllic as it is portrayed today by Arab spokesmen. They were liable to degrading restrictions – though these were not always enforced. It is typical, per- haps, that they suffered particularly from discrimination, pressure and insult in the Yemen, which Professor Goitein has called 'the most Arab of all the Arab countries' (*Jews and Arabs*, p. 73); Jewish orphans were regarded as State property and forcibly converted to Islam (p. 77); Jews were set apart by their dress, and frequently stoned (76).

It may be assumed that the attitude of the Quran, which contains numerous anti-Jewish expressions, especially from the Medina period, had a major influence on the image of the Jews in the eyes of the Arab populace. Special importance may be attributed to sayings that are repeated twice with slight differences in wording: for instance, that

> . . . humiliation and wretchedness were stamped upon them and they were visited with wrath from Allah. (Sura II, 'The Cow,' v. 61; Sura III, 'The Family of 'Imran,' v. 112).

These passages were understood, not as referring to the punishment of the Jews in the time of Moses, but as of wide historical significance: a divine decree, which, as the Arabs understood it, was fulfilled under

historical, political and cultural conditions by lack of political independence and a position of inferiority.

. . .

The Opening to the Quran, which every Muslim repeats in every prayer,
reads:

> Show us the straight path, the path of those whom Thou has
> favoured: not (the path) of those who earn Thine anger nor of those
> who go astray.

According to a common interpretation, though almost certainly not the
original intention, it is the Jews who are meant, for they are rebuked by
God. Al-Jiyar, whose approach is a Muslim one, emphasizes that the
dispersion of the Jews and their continued exile is the will of God, who
never wants them to have a Government (p.–4); in another passage, he
says that their dispersion is an expression of the doom of wretchedness
and humiliation (p. 33).

. . .

The *jizya* tax was not only a source of income but a mark of subordin-
ation and humiliation, and payment was often accompanied with humili-
ating gestures, in keeping with the interpretation of the words of the
Quran:

> Fight against such of those who have been given the Scripture as
> believe not in Allah nor the Last Day . . . until they pay the tribute
> readily, being brought low. (Sura IX, 'Repentance', v. 29).

Muhammad hoped that the Jews would accept his mission, and was
ready to make gestures of goodwill towards them, but when they refused,
he was furious and denounced them vehemently. The existence of the
Jews did not in itself constitute a provocation and an affront to Islam, as it
did to Christendom, particularly as they were recognized as subordinate
and degraded. Since the image of the Jews in Islam was connected with
wretchedness and humiliation, however, the establishment of the State of
Israel as the result of a military victory appeared to be incompatible with
the traditional view. Thus the Quranic image became a matter of
importance.

The inconsistency between the political reality of sovereign independence today and the divine decree of wretchedness seemed to call for

some explanation. Tabbara explains, on the basis of another part of Sura III, 'The Family of 'Imran', v.–112:

> Ignominy shall be their portion wheresoever they are found save (where they grasp) a rope from Allah and a rope from men.

that 'a rope from men' means that the assistance the Jews receive from the Western countries, as a result of which the divine verdict has not been realized, and that 'a rope from Allah' means that God wished the Jews to win their victory so as to draw the attention of the Arab peoples to the corruption that had spread amongst them, so that they should rectify the situation (1966, pp. 45–46).

4.6 Jews and Christians

Thomas Aquinas, 'On the Government of Jews', in A. P. D'Entrèves (ed.), *Aquinas: Selected Political Writings*, ET Oxford, Blackwell, 1948, pp. 85–7, 95

In the first place, then, Your Excellency asked, 'whether at any time, and if so when, it is permissible to exact tribute of the Jews.' To such a question, put thus in general terms, one may reply that it is true, as the Law declares, that Jews, in consequence of their sin, are or were destined to perpetual slavery; so that sovereigns of states may treat their goods as their own property; with the sole proviso that they do not deprive them of all that is necessary to sustain life. But because we must bear ourselves honestly, even to those who are outcasts, lest the name of Christ be blasphemed, (as the Apostle warns us by his own example, to give no offence either to Jews or to Gentiles or to the church of God), it would seem more correct to forego what is permitted by the law, and to abstain from forced loans which it has not been the custom to exact in the past; for what is unaccustomed always rankles more deeply in men's minds. According to this opinion, therefore, you may exact tribute of the Jews according to the custom established by your predecessors, and where there are no other considerations to be taken into account. But, from what I have been able to conjecture, it would seem that your doubts upon this point are heightened by the question you proceed to ask: by the fact, that is, that the Jews in your country appear to possess nothing but what they have acquired by the evil practice of usury. You ask whether it is right to exact from them monies, which in any case should be restored, owing to the way in which they were extorted. The reply to this question would seem to be that although the Jews have no right to retain the money they have extorted from others by usury, neither have you any right to retain it if you take it back from the Jews; except, perhaps, in the case of goods they may have extorted from you yourself or from your predecessors.

. . .

So, to your last question; whether it is correct that all Jews in your realm should be obliged to bear some special sign to distinguish them from Christians. To this the answer is easy and in conformity with the decision given by the General Council. Jews of both sexes and in all Christian lands should on all occasions be distinguished from other people by some particular dress. This is, in any case, imposed upon them by their own law, which ordains that they shall wear a fringe at the four corners of their cloaks to distinguish them from other peoples.

4.7 Toleration and religious freedom

Maurice Cranston, 'John Locke and the Case for Toleration', in Susan Mendus and David Edwards (eds), *On Toleration*, Oxford, Oxford University Press, 1987, pp. 105–8

The great Churches of the world today have moved away from their old mutual intolerance towards the ecumenical ideal, but in the sixteenth century and the seventeenth century confessional divisions were power-ful agents of national discord. In England in the reign of Charles II, disputes around the question of tolerating Roman Catholicism, and especially the question of whether Charles's Roman Catholic brother James should be allowed to accede to the throne, were carrying the kingdom once more to the brink of civil war . . . . It was in exile in Holland that Locke produced his most famous and eloquent contribution to the subject: his Latin *Epistola de tolerantia*, written in November 1685, but not published until 1689.

. . .

Locke himself was a man with deep religious sentiments of his own. So it would not have been enough, or at all appropriate for him, to invoke in this connection the general argument for a natural right to liberty such as he sets forth in his *Second Treatise of Government*. He had to present to Christian readers a Christian case for religious toleration.

. . .

The central theme of Locke's *Epistola de tolerantia* is the radical dis-tinction, as he sees it, between the Church and the State. The state, or commonwealth, he describes as a 'society of men constituted only for the procuring, preserving and advancing their own civil interests'. Civil interests, he goes on to explain, are 'life, liberty, health and indolency of body, and the possession of outward things, such as money, lands, houses, furniture and the like.'

The civil magistrate, as head of the state, has the duty 'by the impartial execution of equal laws' to secure the 'just possession of these things belonging to *this* life'. In order to secure the enforcement of the law, the magistrate is 'armed with the force and strength of all his subjects'. Now Locke insists that 'the whole jurisdiction of the magistrate reaches only to these matters'. Spiritual matters, the care of souls, have nothing to do with him 'because his power consists only in outward force', while 'true and saving religion consists in the inward persuasion of the mind'. The care of souls is the function of the Church. The Church Locke defines as a 'voluntary society of men, joining themselves together of their own accord in order to the public worshipping of God and . . . the salvation of their souls.'

The Church then is voluntary in a sense in which the state is not volun-tary. Locke does not enlarge on this point in this work but we know from his other writings that he regards the state as having originated in a social contract made by our ancestors, which imposes obligations on us even though it is not a contract we have actually made ourselves. The Church is different. 'Nobody is born a member of any Church,' he asserts. 'But everyone joins himself voluntarily to that society in which he has found that profession and worship which is truly acceptable to God.'

Many Christians, of course, would disagree with this description of the Church: but it is a crucial feature of Locke's theory.

The functions of the Church, according to Locke, are:

1 The organisation of public worship.
2 The 'regulation of men's lives according to the rules of virtue and piety'.

In this business of regulating lives, the Church 'may not employ force on any occasion whatever'. Force is the monopoly of the magistrate. The laws of the Church must be imposed by other means, by 'exhortations, admon-itions and advices'; the ultimate sanction being excommunication. No other sanction is permissible. Even excommunication does not deprive a man of his civil rights: for civil rights are not the business of religion.

Correspondingly, religion is not the business of the state. Assuredly, most magistrates do try to enforce religions. But they cannot succeed, Locke says, for while force can make a man go through the outward movements of ritual observance, it cannot compel a man's mind or save a man's soul; it can only produce a hypocrite if it makes a man pretend to conform by outward observance only. Force can never produce that 'faith and inward sincerity' which alone can 'procure acceptance with God'.

C. Henry Peschke, SVD, *Christian Ethics, Volume II: A Presentation of Special Moral Theology in the Light of Vatican II*, Alcester and Dublin, C. Goodliffe Neale, 1978, pp. 305–6

Since within the same state there are frequently various religious groups represented, the question arises which attitude the state should adopt towards them, and especially in which way rulers and government officials, who have their own religious convictions, ought to practise tolerance towards the other religious groups. The teaching of the Catholic Church on this question found an explicit reformulation in the 'Declaration on Religious Freedom' (DH) by Vatican II.

Though the Second Vatican Council expresses its belief that the 'one true religion subsists in the Catholic and apostolic Church, to which the Lord Jesus committed the duty of spreading it abroad among all men', it likewise expresses its conviction that it is upon the human conscience that the obligation falls to seek the truth, especially in what concerns God and his Church, and to embrace the truth it comes to know (DH 1). 'It is one of the major tenets of Catholic doctrine that man's response to God in faith must be free. Therefore no one is to be forced to embrace the Christian faith against his own will. This doctrine is contained in the Word of God and it was constantly proclaimed by the Fathers of the Church' (DH 10).

Therefore 'all men are to be immune from coercion on the part of individuals or of social groups and of any human power, in such wise that in matters religious no one is to be forced to act in a manner contrary to his own beliefs. Nor is anyone to be restrained from acting in accordance with his own beliefs, whether privately or publicly . . . This right of the human person to religious freedom is to be recognized in the constitutional law whereby society is governed. Thus it is to become a civil right' (DH 2).

Religious freedom does not only include the right for all religious bodies to worship God privately or publicly, but also the right to public teaching and witness to the respective faith. According to the Declaration on Religious Freedom, the same freedom which the Church claims for herself is to be granted to religious bodies of every kind (DH 4).

Only in the case where a religious group commits abuses on pretext of freedom of religion has the state the right and duty to intervene. 'It is the special duty of government to provide this protection. However, government is not to act in arbitrary fashion or in an unfair spirit of partisanship. Its action is to be controlled by juridical norms which are in conformity with the objective moral order' (DH 7).

Thus, by way of a conclusion, the religious tolerance taught by Vatican II is not an indifferentism which regards all the different religions and denominations as equally true or false. It is the firm belief of the Council that the true religion subsists in the Catholic Church. But in the public, civil life the subjective convictions of every citizen and of the different religious groups have to be respected as long as they do not imperil the common weal, and the same rights of religious freedom have to be granted to everybody.

4.8 Approaching other faiths

Max Warren, General Introduction to the *Christian Presence* series of books, London, SCM, 1961 onwards

Our first task in approaching another people, another culture, another religion, is to take off our shoes, for the place we are approaching is holy. Else we may find ourselves treading on men's dreams. More serious still, we may forget that God was here before our arrival. We have, then, to ask what is the authentic religious content in the experience of the Muslim, the Hindu, the Buddhist or whoever he may be. We may, if we have asked humbly and respectfully, still reach the conclusion that our brothers have started from a false premise and reached a faulty conclusion. But we must not arrive at our judgment from outside their religious situation. We have to try to sit where they sit, to enter sympathetically into the pains and griefs and joys of their history and see how those pains and griefs and joys have determined the premises of their argument. We have, in a word, to be 'present' with them.

Max Warren, *Partnership: The Study of an Idea*, London, SCM, 1956, pp. 85–90

The starting point for any assessment of the present relationship between the peoples of Asia and Africa and those of the West is the recognition that there is a profound revolt of the former against the latter. This is frequently disguised by the avidity with which in both Asia and Africa the techniques and skills of the West are coveted. The gas station and the cinema and the radio spread a thin patina of westernization over the remotest communities.

. . .

Accepting, then, the reality of the urge for independence and allowing it full value, I would suggest three factors which lie below the surface and provide the dynamic, often largely unconscious, behind the social and political movements of our time.

The *first* of these is the discovery of a new self-respect on the part of the peoples of Asia and Africa, a sense of worth which, be it noted has been the inspiration of the movements for independence and *not* their sequel, though obviously enough the achievement of independence greatly enhances this awareness.

. . .

Behind this discovery I discern two influences, one steadily at work over a period, one much more sudden in its impact and likely to be less enduring. The first of these is the slow permeation of the Christian view of the worth of the individual. Without attempting to elaborate what at first sight may seem a surprising suggestion I would content myself with indicating the following points. The Christian gospel about God's concern for man to the point of involvement, responsibility, and liability was not only proclaimed in an Asia and Africa in which these ideas were new, but it was demonstrated there. Concern for the under-privileged and the out-caste, the unwanted and the orphan, the leper and the blind came as a direct result of the gospel. A new attitude to woman was another direct result of the gospel. It is only necessary to think of the education of girls, and one result of this in the nursing profession in Asia and Africa, to appreciate that a revolutionary force was at work before the first Asian or African had begun to dream of independence. When we go on to consider the general impact of education modelled on the Christian education of the West, an education whose purpose is the development of responsible citizenship, we are not far from the source of those ideas whose inherent logic made independence movements quite inevitable. There remains to note the introduction of a conception of law before which all men are equal, a conception which in the West, for all its Roman ancestry, was developed and made effective under Christian inspiration. The slow but steady permeation of this idea of personal worth is the concealed source of the great revolution of construction of our time.

The tragic paradox, itself in no small measure responsible for this concealment, is to be found in the disillusionment of the East and Africa with the West's betrayal of its own spiritual heritage. This betrayal, beginning with the attitude of contempt for the Asian and African on the part of individuals from the West, has been, beyond question, the main source behind the bitterness which has characterized so much of the struggle for independence.

. . .

When to this arrogance on the part of all too many there was added the spectacle of the White Man's suicidal loss of self-control in two world wars, the disillusionment was complete. With this disillusionment went a sharp reaction against the acceptance of the religion which appeared to be so indissoluble a part of the fabric of the West, a tendency to ignore the reality of that religious contribution to the new Asia and the new Africa and a revival, in one form or another, of the old traditional religions.

If the Christian view of the worth of the individual is the first of the dynamic factors behind the contemporary scene in Asia and Africa, the second is the penetrating influence of the new found conviction that man can control his environment. This discovery has profoundly altered the Asian scene and in a rather different way the African. It has brought a re-birth of hope to millions whose lives had been previously dominated by the old religious concepts of fate, *karma*, and the non-reality of material things.

. . .

One factor remains to be noted, whose dynamic force will be variously assessed, but which must not be ignored. The growth of population in both Asia and Africa is proceeding at a pace which already threatens multitudes with death by starvation, because the pace at which the world's food production is going up is not matching the rate of population growth. This is a factor which adds urgency to every political situation in Asia and Africa. It is, what is more, a factor which will increasingly determine the shape of national policies in these areas. Let those who are most exasperated by the neutralist attitude of the independent people of Asia be warned that this neutralism will not endure much longer. It will be exchanged for co-operation with whichever power *bloc* offers the best prospects of dealing rapidly with the stark realities of famine.

. . .

Perhaps our first task is to see ourselves as others see us. We who come out of a culture which has been profoundly influenced by the Christian faith, whose concept of law and of politics derives from Christian insights, whose whole basic attitude to the material universe is based on the Christian doctrine of creation, are apt to be quite unaware of the degree to which this inner core of Christian conviction is mediated to other peoples of other cultures with the tacit assumption that all the trimmings which go with these convictions are equally part of the gospel. This insensitiveness to the values of other cultures, this presumption of the infinite superiority at every point of our own culture, is a form of implied contempt. This is a form of spiritual imperialism, and Asia and Africa do not like it any more than they like other imperialisms.

Closely allied to this is a characteristic very common to us of the West of a certain impatient aggressive benevolence. Philip Leon . . . deals in one passage with the reactions provoked by the exercise of benevolent power. He reminds those who possess the power to be benevolent that the frequent ingratitude which seems so graceless a sequel to the benevolence is not due to an additional dose of original sin. He says, and we do well to ponder what he says:

> The ingrate is not in love with crookedness or evil; but the hand that feeds is as wounding to his pride as the hand that strikes: his imagination soon identifies the one with the other, and he retaliates accordingly.

4.9 Anonymous Christians?

Karl Rahner, *Theological Investigations,* **Volume V, ET London, Darton, Longman & Todd, 1966, pp. 118–21, 126–7, 131, 133–4**

1st Thesis: We must begin with the thesis which follows, because it certainly represents the basis in the Christian faith of the theological understanding of other religions. This thesis states that Christianity understands itself as the absolute religion, intended for all men, which cannot recognize any other religion beside itself as of equal right. . . . *This* relationship of God to man is basically the same for all men, because it rests on the Incarnation, death and resurrection of the one Word of God become flesh. Christianity is God's own interpretation in his Word of this relationship of God to man founded in Christ by God himself.

. . .

Nevertheless, the Christian religion as such has a beginning in history; it did not always exist but began at some point in time. It has not always and everywhere been *the* way of salvation for men – at least not in its historically tangible ecclesio-sociological constitution and in the reflex fruition of God's saving activity in, and in view of, Christ. As a historical quantity Christianity has, therefore, a temporal and spatial starting point in Jesus of Nazareth and in the saving event of the unique Cross and the empty tomb in Jerusalem. It follows from this, however, that this absolute religion – even when it begins to be this for practically all men – must come in a historical way to men, facing them as the only legitimate and demanding religion for them. It is therefore a question of whether this moment, when the existentially real demand is made by the absolute religion in its historically tangible form, takes place really at the same chronological moment for all men, or whether the occurrence of this moment has itself a history and thus is not chronologically simultaneous for all men, cultures and spaces of history.

. . .

From this there follows a delicately differentiated understanding of our first thesis: we maintain positively only that, as regards destination, Christianity is the absolute and hence the only religion for all men. We leave it, however, an open question (at least in principle) at what exact point in time the absolute obligation of the Christian religion has in fact come into effect for every man and culture.

. . .

2nd Thesis: Until the moment when the gospel really enters into the historical situation of an individual, a non-Christian religion (even outside the Mosaic religion) does not merely contain elements of a natural know-ledge of God, elements, moreover, mixed up with human depravity which is the result of original sin and later aberrations. It contains also super-natural elements arising out of the grace which is given to men as a gratuitous gift on account of Christ. For this reason a non-Christian religion can be recognized as a *lawful* religion (although only in different degrees) without thereby denying the error and depravity contained in it.

. . .

The Holy Scriptures do indeed give us the official and valid deposit to help us differentiate among the spirits which moved the history of the Old Testament religion. But since the infallible delimitation of the canon of the Old Testament is again to be found only in the New Testament, the exact and final differentiation between the lawful and the unlawful in the Old Testament religion is again possible only by making use of the New

Testament as something eschatologically final. The unity of the concrete religion of the Old Testament, which (ultimately) could be distinguished only gropingly and at one's own risk, was, however, the unity willed by God, providential for the Israelites in the order of salvation and indeed the lawful religion for them. In this connection it must furthermore be taken into consideration that it was meant to be this only for the Israelites and for no one else; the institution of those belonging to the Jewish religion without being of the Jewish race, (i.e. of the proselytes) was a very much later phenomenon. Hence it cannot be a part of the notion of a lawful religion in the above sense that it should be free from corruption, error and objective moral wrong in the concrete form of its appearance, or that it should contain a clear objective and permanent final court of appeal for the conscience of the individual to enable the individual to differentiate clearly and with certainty between the elements willed and instituted by God and those which are merely human and corrupt.

. . .

3rd Thesis: If the second thesis is correct, then Christianity does not simply confront the member of an extra-Christian religion as a mere non-Christian but as someone who can and must already be regarded in this or that respect as an anonymous Christian. It would be wrong to regard the pagan as someone who has not yet been touched in any way by God's grace and truth. If, however, he has experienced the grace of God – if, in certain circumstances, he has already accepted this grace as the ultimate, unfathomable entelechy of his existence by accepting the immeasurableness of his dying existence as opening out into infinity – then he has already been given revelation in a true sense even before he has been affected by missionary preaching from without.

. . .

4th Thesis: It is possibly too much to hope, on the one hand, that the religious pluralism which exists in the concrete situation of Christians will disappear in the foreseeable future. On the other hand, it is nevertheless absolutely permissible for the Christian himself to interpret this non-Christianity as Christianity of an anonymous kind which he does always still go out to meet as a missionary, seeing it as a world which is to be brought to the explicit consciousness of what already belongs to it as a divine offer or already pertains to it also over and above this as a divine gift of grace accepted unreflectedly and implicitly. If both these statements are true, then the Church will not so much regard herself today as the exclusive community of those who have a claim to salvation but rather as the historically tangible vanguard and the historically and socially constituted explicit expression of what the Christian hopes is present as a hidden reality even outside the visible Church.

. . .

The Church will go out to meet the non-Christian of tomorrow with the attitude expressed by St Paul when he said: What therefore you do not know and yet worship (and yet *worship*!) that I proclaim to you (Acts 17.23). On such a basis one can be tolerant, humble and yet firm towards all non-Christian religions.

4.10 Religion and genocide: The continuing issue

Michael A. Sells, 'Bosnia: Some Dimensions of Genocide', *Religious Studies News*, 9, 2, 1994, pp. 4–5

April in Bosnia marked the second anniversary of what we have come to know as 'ethnic cleansing.' Aspects of the Bosnia tragedy such as the siege of Sarajevo have captured world attention. Widely misunderstood, however, is the true extent of the 'ethnic cleansing' and its fundamentally religious character. In this essay I will examine some of the religious dimensions of this genocidal activity in order to get past the usual accounts which rarely do more than generalize about 'age-old tensions.'

All major Bosnian populations (Serb, Muslim and Croat) trace their descent from the same south Slavic tribes, and (despite protestations of nationalists) all speak the same language. The term 'ethnic' in 'ethnic cleansing' actually refers to religious affiliation. The testimony in the UN War Crimes Commission reports suggests that what is (according to Webster's Ninth) called 'cleansing' is actually genocide, i.e. 'the deliberate and systematic destruction of a racial, political, or cultural group.' While it is true that there have been 'abuses on all sides', as in most conflicts, the vast majority of victims have been unarmed Bosnian Muslim civilians. An estimated 200,000 Bosnian Muslims have been killed (out of a pre-war Bosnian total population of some 4 million).

The ethnic cleansing consists of: 1) Attacks on lightly defended settlements by heavily armed forces; 2) Shelling of settlements that resist; 3) Daily mass-killings, torture and starvation; 4) Systematic rapes; 5) Annihilation of cultural heritage (mosques, libraries, schools, museums, cemeteries, manuscript collections); 6) An economy of pillage with regular 'caravans' of Muslim loot taken across the Drina river into Serbia proper and; 7) Final ritualized dehumanisation in which survivors are stripped of every personal possession.

The treatment of Bosnian Muslims as an 'ethnic group' is usually traced to the 1971 Yugoslav constitutional establishment of Bosnian Muslims as a Yugoslav 'nationality.' However, both the identification of religions with 'ethnicity' and the notion of 'cleansing' have far deeper roots in the religious ideology of a nationalist Christoslavism which maintains that Slavs are by nature, Christian. Any deviation from Christianity, therefore, is perceived as race-betrayal. We cannot hope to understand genocide in Europe unless we understand this religious ideology. To do so, it helps to examine the mythology and literature that both shapes and represents Serbian attitudes toward Bosnian Muslims.

The Kosovo myth: Slavic Muslims portrayed as Christ-killers in *The Mountain Wreath*

In 1389, the Serb Prince Lazar was defeated and killed in a battle against Ottoman Turkish Sultan Murad II on the plain of Kosovo. While historians dispute the significance of the battle, in Serbian Mythology it entailed the loss of Serb independence, a loss that was represented in cosmic terms. Lazar is portrayed as a Christ figure. He has a Last Supper with 12 Nobles, one of whom, Vuk Brankovic, is a traitor and gives the battle plans to the Turks. During the battle, the Christ-Prince Lazar is slain and with him dies the Serb nation, to rise again only with the resurrection of Lazar. Turks are thus equated with Christ-Killers and Vuk Brankovic, the 'Turk within,' becomes a symbol (and ancestral curse) of all Slavic Muslims.

Thus the same manipulation of the 'Christ-killer' charge used in the persecutions of Jews from the First Crusade in 1096 has formed the rationale for the persecution of Slavic Muslims. A Classic illustration of this rationale can be seen in the play, *The Mountain Wreath*, written by Prince Bishop Petar II, known by the pen-name of Njegos, which portrays the 18th century Montenegrin extermination of Slavic Muslims (*Istraga Poturica*).

The drama opens with Bishop Danilo, the play's protagonist, brooding on the evil of Islam, the tragedy of Kosovo, and the treason of Vuk Brankovic. Danilo's warriors suggest celebrating the holy day (Pentecost) by 'cleansing' (*cistimo*) the land of non-Christians (v. 95). The chorus chants: 'the high mountains reek with the stench of non-Christians [v. 284].' One of Danilo's men proclaims that the struggle won't come to an end until 'we or the Turks [Slavic Muslims] are exterminated.' The reference to the Slavic Muslims as 'Turks' crystallizes the view that by converting to Islam they have changed their racial identity and become the Turks who killed the Christ-Prince Lazar.

While the killing in Bosnia has often been misrepresented as a 'blood feud,' in The *Mountain Wreath* such genocide is explicitly placed *outside* of the blood feud. In tribal Montenegro and Serbia, a godfather (*Kuma*) ceremony was used to reconcile clans who had fallen into blood-feud. But in *The Mountain Wreath*, when Muslims suggest a Kuma reconciliation, Danilo's men object that the Kuma ceremony requires baptism. The Muslims offer an ecumenical analogy, suggesting that the Muslim Hair-cutting ceremony is a parallel in their tradition to baptism. Danilo's men respond with a stream of scatological insults, the chorus chants *Tako, Vec Nikako* (this way; there is no other) to indicate the 'act' that must be taken. The play ends with the triumphant extermination of Slavic Muslims as a formal initiation of Serb nationhood.

By moving the conflict from the realm of blood feud into a cosmic duality of good and evil, Njegos placed Slavic Muslims in a permanent state of otherness. The sympathetic qualities of the Muslims are the last temptation of Danilo. However sympathetic in person, Muslims are ultimately viewed as Christ-killers, 'blasphemers,' 'spitters on the cross.' After slaughtering the Muslims – man, woman, and child – the Serb warriors take communion without the confession that was mandatory after blood-vengeance.

The Mountain Wreath is memorized and quoted by radical Serb nationalists today. In Bosnia, nationalist Serb 'ethnic cleansers' wear patches depicting the battle of Kosovo. In 1966 Miovan Djilas, one of *The Mountain Wreath*'s admirers, argued that the historical extermination of the Montenegrin Muslims was a 'process' rather than a single 'event,' and that Bishop Petar shaped it into a single act for literary and ideological purposes. While there is doubt whether the *Istraga Poturica* occurred as a single event in the late 18th century, the eight U.S. reports to the War Crimes Commission and the two Helsinki Watch Reports (War Crimes in Bosnia-Hercegovina, vol. 1, 1992, and vol. 2, 1993) suggest that it occurred in 1992–93.

In 1989, three million Serb pilgrims streamed into Kosovo for the Passion Play commemoration of the 600th anniversary of the battle of Kosovo. On this occasion, Serb President Slobodan Milosevic announced his change from communist apparachnik to champion of Serbdom. Those who directed the Passion Play, who acted in it and who sat in the first rows in 1989, were carrying out the first genocidal policies against Bosnian civilians three years later. Just as Good Friday remembrances of the passion of Christ were used by anti-Semites to foment attacks on Jews, so the Kosovo Passion Play (which puts the Slavic Muslims in the position of 'Christ-killers') became an occasion for persecution.

Christoslavism in the work of Ivo Andric

'Race-betrayal' is a major theme of *The Mountain Wreath* and the strand of Serbian Literature it represents. By converting to Islam, Njegos insisted, Slavic Muslims became 'Turks.' The novelist Ivo Andric, a hero to both Serb and Croat nationalists who have been 'cleansing' Muslims from Bosnia, re-presents this race-conversion in clear ideological terms. He begins by grounding his position in the work of Njegos when he writes: *'Njegos, who can always be counted on for the truest expression of the people's mode of thinking and apprehending, portrays in his terse and plastic manner the process of conversion thus: "The lions* [i.e. those who remained Christian according to Andric's footnote] *turned into tillers of the soil, / the cowardly and covetous turned into Turks."'* By affirming Njegos' description and appealing to it as the message of 'the people,' Andric gives a historical rationale for defining Bosnian Muslims as not part of the people.

For Andric, the ancient Bosnian Church, persecuted as heretical by both Catholic and Orthodox forces, was a sign of a 'young Slavic race' still torn between 'heathen concepts with dualistic coloring and unclear Christian dogmas.' Most Bosnians believe that the members of the ancient Bosnian Church, called Bogmils or Patarins, were the ancestors of the Bosnian Muslims. Andric portrays Bosnian Muslims not only as cowardly and covetous and the 'heathen element of a young race,' but finally as the corrupted 'Orient' that cut off the Slavic race from the 'civilising currents' of the West.

Andric's most famous novel, *The Bridge on the Drina*, centres on a bridge on the Drina River that was commissioned by Mehmet Pasha Sukolovic (a Serb who had been taken to Istanbul to become a Pasha). To appease fairies (*vila*) holding up the bridge's construction, the builders must wall up two Christian infants within it. Two holes that appear in the bridge are interpreted as the place where the infants' mothers come to suckle their children. The story crystallizes the view that an essentially Christic race of Slavs is walled up within the encrustation of an alien religion. It also represents an obsession with the Ottoman practice of selecting Serb boys (such as Sukolovic) to be sent to Istanbul, brought up Muslim, and trained for high positions. Such people, however successful they become, are perceived as perpetual exiles to themselves, cut off from the Christian essence of their Slavic souls.

This brief reading of Njegos and Andric cannot do justice to the range of their work, nor is it meant to explain the genocide in Bosnia. It is meant only to illustrate that religion (despite frequent denials) is indeed a powerful and operative element in the tragedy.

Responding to Religious Cleansing in Bosnia

Last winter, Russian neo-nazi Vladimir Zhirinovsky visited the highest ranking surviving SS officer in Germany, and then went to Serb-occupied Bosnia, where he was welcomed by Bosnian Serb ethnonationalists. While it would be wrong to equate the genocide in Bosnia with the Holocaust, it is equally wrong to ignore the moral implications of genocide in Europe, against a non-Christian population, especially on the 50th anniversary of the Holocaust. Some governmental and church leaders in the region and in the international community have failed to respond to the Bosnian Muslim calls for assistance. More disturbing has been the active support by Serbian religious leaders of those Serbian military and governmental officials who are responsible for designing and implementing the policy of 'ethnic cleansing.'

For example, Metropolitan Nikolaj, the highest ranking Serb Church official in Bosnia, stood between General Ratko Mladic and Bosnian Serb President Radovan Karadzic – architects of the ethnic cleansing – and spoke of the Bosnian Serbs' struggle as following the 'hard road of Christ.' Serbian priests have blessed militias on their return from kill-and-plunder expeditions and waved incense over a boxing match put on by the warlord (a criminal known as 'Arkan') associated with the worst atrocities against Muslims. Ethnonationalists celebrated the feast of St Sava, founder of the Serbian Church, by burning down the 300-year-old mosque at Trebinje and massacring the town's Muslims. The mayor of Zvornik (a previously Muslim majority city) celebrated the completion of 'ethnic cleansing' and the town's new status as one hundred percent Muslim-free by erecting a new Church to St Stepan and kissing a crucifix. Serbian Church leaders in America have vilified Muslims and have refused to condemn the systematic ethnic cleansing of the Bosnian Serb government.

Immediately after the Sarajevo Market Massacre, the National Council of Churches, which has been reticent in speaking out on Bosnia, wrote to President Clinton praising 'restraint' in the use of force. For two years, a civilian Muslim populace was 'cleansed,' with a kill rate (number of people killed per day as a percentage of total population) that may equal that of WW2 Nazi occupation in Bosnia. The killing was carried out with a UN arms embargo against the victims, little effort to disarm the aggressors, in front of the largest military alliance in the history of humankind. The UN showed 'restraint' by refusing to enforce some 30 resolutions forbidding the shelling of civilians, abuse in detention camps, interference with food convoys, and attacks on safe havens. A language of complicity was developed, with half-truths (at best) such as 'age-old ethnic antagonisms,' 'civil war,' 'blame on all sides' used to justify restraint in the face of genocide and interpreted (correctly) by the aggressors as a green light for more ethnic cleansing. After the Market Massacre, the United States and the UN ran out of restraint and enforced a resolution. The shelling of Sarajevo stopped.

Despite the generous actions of individual Christians, charges of inaction have been levelled at organized Church bodies. Given the religious aspect of the conflict and the history of genocide in Europe, many will be listening to the Churches' response to issues still posed by 'ethnic cleansing' in Bosnia. Will religious leaders indirectly endorse ethnic cleansing by supporting a peace settlement that rewards it? Will they argue that the perpetrators be held accountable? Will they act to help ensure that the victims (many of whom are now being held in inhuman conditions in European refugee camps) be treated with humanity? Will they continue to acquiesce to the use of Jesus' name to authorize this activity?

As scholars of religion, we commonly study how religions bind together communities, offer a framework for moral decisions, relate ethos and world view, and guide inquiry into fundamental questions of human existence. Religions can also be used to authorize the most inhuman behavior. The acceptance of the term 'ethnic cleansing' is a sign of a widespread desire to deny this latter aspect of religion. In a post cold-war world of increasing religious militancies, an examination of religion and genocide may be one of our more pressing priorities, despite the discomfort it engenders.

4.11 Some explanatory notes on Islam

Ann Loades and Michael Ipgrave

Prophets in Islam

Nabi: Prophets. One tradition reports that 124,000 prophets have been sent to the world. There is no people to whom a prophet has not been sent. They are always secondary to the message they bring. They are full of Barakah – the blessing of God. The following are key prophets:

Ibrahim: Abraham. He protested against the idolatry of his father's house. His willingness to sacrifice his son was a sign of submission. The Muslim tradition is of course based on the Qur'anic text (Surah 37), where the lad is not named. Most commentators explain that the birth of Isaac is the reward for Abraham's obedience and that the older Ishmael was the intended sacrifice.

Musa: Moses. He knew the law of God, but it was corrupted in later Jewish tradition.

'Isa: Jesus. He was born of a virgin and is associated with the spirit of God. He proclaimed a message of divine love and unity. He was not crucified, but was taken by God to Himself. Later corruptions – the cruci- fixion, and Son of God and Trinitarian language – denigrate the original purity of his message. His gospel was lost, though elements survive in the Christian gospels, such as the stress on love, obedience to God, and the Sermon on the Mount. Mary's virginity signifies preparedness, the availability of the messenger, and the purity of the revelation. In this respect, the Virgin Mary, bearer of the Word of God, can be likened to the unlettered Prophet Muhammad, vehicle of God's revealed word.

Muhammad: The seal of prophecy. He was not 'lettered', and the Qur'an (the word of God) was dictated 'into his soul' by the archangel Gabriel in one night and then was successively revealed through him as occasion demanded. The text is non-negotiable as the 'uncreated' word of God in Arabic. Written down within a generation, variant versions were des- troyed so that only one text survived. A 'translation' of it is deemed to be akin to a paraphrase or commentary.

The life of Muhammad

570: Muhammad was born in Makkah (Mecca), a great trading centre and caravan junction. It had a sanctuary (Ka'aba) and in it, a stone which was linked to Ibrahim. There were Jews and Christians in Makkah at this time. The Christians were likely to be either Nestorian (who emphasised the *man* Jesus, only loosely connected with the divine) or Monophysite (who emphasised Jesus' divine nature subsuming his human nature). Muhammad was born to a widowed mother and brought up by an extended family.

610: One night during the month of Ramadan, the Qur'an was revealed in a cave (Hira') on a mountain near Makkah. This is known as the Laylat al-Qadr, the night of power. Muhammad heard the voice of Gabriel commanding him to recite the creation of humanity from a clot of blood: 'Recite: In the Name of thy Lord who created, created Man of a blood-clot. / Recite: And thy Lord is the Most Generous who taught by the Pen, taught Man that he knew not.' (Surah 96, 1–5. Taken from A. J. Arberry, *The Koran Interpreted*, Oxford, Oxford University Press, 1983, p. 651)

613: The beginning of the Prophet's public proclamation. His message centred on the unity of God, the falseness of idols, and a summons to fair dealing. His message was received warmly by Ethiopians and Christians; Jews were less enthusiastic. Christians provided refuge from persecution for the earliest Muslims.

620: Mi'raj. The Prophet was transported to a 'further mosque' in Jerusalem (which is now the Dome of the Rock) and from there to the presence of God, after which he returned to Makkah. From the prophet's journey to heaven (ascent of his soul or of him literally – interpretations differ), cosmologies developed.

622: Hijrah. The emigration. The prophet left Makkah for Madinah (Medina) when invited by the citizens of that city. All dates in Islam work from 622 CE (A.H.). Within his lifetime, he established not just a 'faith community', but a polity, a city/state. He formed a pact with *all* people of Madinah, including Jews and Christians, who were recognised as worshipping the one God (with their own scriptures – hence the name 'People of the Book'). These had protection within Muslim polity. This became the pattern for later practice.

624: Breach with Jewish tribes. The Prophet was banished from Madinah, so the direction of prayer was altered: away from Jerusalem and the Temple Mount, towards Makkah and the Ka'aba. Qiblah: The direction of prayer.

630: Conquest of Makkah unopposed. The Prophet purified the Ka'aba of idols. One of the pictures on the walls at Makkah – Mary holding Jesus – was protected by Muhammad, though it was later removed.

632: The prophet died at Madinah, where he was buried. Leadership is taken on by a Khalif (successor) who is not a prophet. The first five are *chosen* by the community. Later it became a hereditary office.

Key Concepts in Islamic Law and Community

Shari'ah: Islamic law. It has four sources: 1) Qur'an; 2) Sunnah; 3) Ijma – consensus of the community (effectively, of the legal scholars); and 4) Ijtihad – effort – adapting the law to new situations. The Mongol invasions of the 13th century resulted in a loss of confidence and therefore, the 'Closing of the gates of Ijtihad'. Only towards the end of the 19th century do some try to re-establish the legitimacy of 'opening the gates'. This is a continuing source of controversy.

Haram: A concept which developed perhaps as early as the Prophet's lifetime. It refused entry into Madinah and Makkah to all non-Muslims. The present Saudi government has extended haram (in the sense of prohibition of non-Muslim religions) to the whole state. This extension is based on a hadith attributed to the Prophet on his deathbed.

Ummah: The Islamic community. It is the world-wide brotherhood of the faithful which binds Muslims together through the law of God which both confers privileges on them and requires duties from them in return.

Sunni and Shi'a: The Sunnis (from Sunnah – tradition of the Prophet) ironically were those who wanted the choice of successors of Muhammad, though within thirty years the succession became hereditary. The Shi'ites (meaning party of the people) wanted Ali, the Prophet's son-in-law. When the grandson of the Prophet, Hussein, was killed in battle, there developed a Shi'ite tradition of memorial of this event every year. Shi'a has become the religion of a minority, but is dominant in Iranian / Persian culture. This Iranian form has its own legal method, but the Shi'ites still make pilgrimage to Makkah (hajj). The Ismailis are a distinctive group of Shi'ites which developed over the centuries to protect themselves from Sunni persecution (hence their culture of concealment). The problem about them for other Muslims is that they believe that the light of God is manifest in Ali and his descendants. This is far too close to *shirk*. The Aga Khan is the hereditary leader of the Ismaili community.

The Five Pillars of Islam

1) Shahadah: The confession of faith

'There is no God but Allah and Muhammad is the messenger of God'

This confession works both by way of denial and affirmation. Different traditions in Islam have stressed either denial or affirmation.

Denial: 'There is no "so-called" god but God', the point being to set human beings free from bondage to false and dangerous idols. There is no analogy/reflection of God in creation. There is great stress on the utter transcendence of God in Islam. There was in the 18th century a Saudi Arabian sect, the Wahhabi, concerned with practical reform, who strongly criticised the 'cult' of Muhammad and some Muslim saints as a dangerous practice. Among their descendants are the present Saudi royal family.

Affirmation: There is no reality which is unrelated to the one reality of God. Tawhid (unity) all things cohere; all things stem from God. The Sufi (mystical) strand in Islam take a positive view of the relation of creator and creatures.

2) Salat (Salah): Canonical or ritual prayer, made five times a day from the age of reason. It is preceded by ablutions, and can take place anywhere which is physically clean and free of idols. Prostration is of the essence of prayer and is made facing Makkah. The worshippers are lined up in rows behind the Imam, or leader. For men, prayer is preferably performed together in the mosque, and of special importance is the Friday *midday* prayer. The times are morning, middle of the day, late afternoon, about sunset and night. It is forbidden to have these prayers exactly at sunrise, high noon and sunset, because of the danger of sun-worship. Individual supplications are also important, as for some is the mystical remembrance of God. Tradition holds that the Prophet was taught the fivefold salat by Gabriel during his Mi'raj.

Men and women in prayer channel through themselves the rhythm of the whole universe. Women often pray at home, though some mosques have a women's gallery. They are separated from the men to avoid unseemly behaviour and distraction. Both intention and prayer purify a place and the individual worshipper. Muslims also make ablutions before reading the Qur'an.

3) Zakat: Almsgiving. A voluntary tax amounting to 2½ percent of one's assets (e.g. jewellery and property) per year, excluding property in which one lives. The money goes to support the poor or suffering members of the Muslim community. During Ramadan, much more is given. There are also collections in the mosque on a Friday, when the sermon may focus on the present-day situation in the Muslim community.

4) Sawm: Fasting during the month of Ramadan (as the month is 30 days, following the lunar calendar, this period moves around the year). From

sunrise to sunset no food or drink (or cigarettes or sex) is allowed, so it depends on the time of year and length of days as to how severe the fast is. It is not necessary for the sick, travellers, young children or pregnant women. As it is a special expression of dependence on God and of the unity of the community there is great concern if there is disagreement about the dates of Ramadan. Eid or 'Id marks the end of Ramadan. 'Id al-Fitr depends on sighting of the new moon. It is a time marked by feasts and special meals.

5) Hajj: Pilgrimage to Makkah, if one can make arrangements for dependants. It is associated with traditions of Ibrahim in the Qur'an, with a goat killed instead of Ishmael. Muslims world wide join in this sacrifice on 'Id ul-Adha.

6) Some add a sixth pillar – Jihad. This is the struggle for righteousness, not least when the Muslim is under attack. Whether this is undertaken depends on the opinions of qualified Muslim Jurists.

Key terms in Islam

Shirk: The most serious sin. It is the association of God and creatures; putting something else alongside God. For instance, the language of divine sonship or God as Father is un-Islamic.

Shahadah: Witness, in the sense of 1) what one sees; and 2) bearing witness.

Shahid-a: A person who bears witness. It also means 'martyr'.

There is stress on how human beings know, serve, meditate on and remember God, so there are names of God. Dhikr: Remembrance. Most popular in the Sufi/mystical strand. Ayat: Creation is full of *signs* which aid in remembrance.

Islam: Submission to the one Lord.

Muslim: One who has made his act of submission.

Rasul: A messenger who comes to the world with a message (which is in itself mercy). Muhammad is the messenger of God.

Sunnah: The tradition of the Prophet (Muhammad).

Hadith: Opinion of the Prophet; i.e. a particular tradition's recording of the Prophet's words or actions. Unlike the Qur'an, it is open for criticism and there are tests of the authenticity of different traditions relying on the establishment of a chain of transmission through respectable witnesses.

Da'wah: Literally, invitation. Fulfilment of the commandment to 'call men unto the path of Allah'. Da'wah rests both on express scriptural injunction, and on the fact that the message itself demands a wider telling.

Topics for discussion

1 What is meant by *jihad* in the Islamic tradition? What similarities and differences do you detect between *jihad* and (a) biblical attitudes to war, (b) the Christian just war tradition?

2 To what extent is it appropriate to describe traditional Muslim attitudes to Jewish and Christian minorities in their midst as 'tolerance'? Does tolerance simply imply the absence of force, or does it require equality of treatment?

3 What is the relation between tolerance and peace? Do both simply imply absence of conflict, or something more?

4 On what religious and/or moral principles should tolerance be based: e.g. respect for the individual, respect for conscience, the fact that true faith cannot be forced?

5 What implications has the acceptance of tolerance for the practice of Christian mission? To what extent did Christian mission in the past enhance or undermine the unique worth Christians believe attaches to individual human beings?

6 Does tolerance require one to regard all religions as of equal value? Is there any way of treating the belief of another religion with respect in a way that does not undermine the status of one's own beliefs?

7 With reference to either (a) just war theory or (b) *jihad*, respond to the claim that 'religion propagates war'.

Acknowledgements

T & T Clark for quotations from 'Christian Ethics: The Contemporary Context' by David Brown in *New Occasions Teach New Duties? Christian Ethics for Today* edited by C.S. Rodd; Hodder & Stoughton and Westminster John Knox Press for quotations from *Dliemmas: A Christian Approach to Moral Decision Making* by Richard Higginson; Blackwell Publishers Ltd for quotations from *The Use of the Bible in Christian Ethics* by Thomas W. Ogletree, *Choices: Ethics and the Christian* by David Brown and 'On the Government of Jews' by Thomas Aquinas in *Aquinas: Selected Political Writings* edited by A.P. D'Entrèves; Penguin Books Ltd for quotations from *Aquinas: An Introduction to the Life and Work of the Great Medieval Thinker* by F.C. Copleston copyright © F.C. Copleston 1955 and *The Koran* translated by N.J. Dawood (Penguin Classics 1956, 5th revised edn 1990) copyright © N.J. Dawood 1956, 1959, 1966, 1968, 1974, 1990; Augsburg Fortress Press for a quotation from 'The Use of the Bible in Christian Ethics' by Bruce Birch and Larry Rasmussen in *The Bible and Ethics in the Christian Life* edited by Ronald P. Hamel and Kenneth R. Himes OFM; University of Notre Dame Press for quotations from *Directions in Fundamental Moral Theology* by Charles E. Curran; SCM Press and University of Notre Dame Press for quotations from *The Peaceable Kingdom: A Primer in Christian Ethics* by Stanley Hauerwas copyright 1984 by University of Notre Dame Press; The Lutterworth Press for a quotation from *The New Testament Basis of Pacifism* by G.H.C. MacGregor; SCM Press for quotations from *Basic Christian Ethics* by Paul Ramsey, the General Introduction by Max Warren to the 'Christian Presence' series and *Partnership: The Study of an Idea* by Max Warren; *Interpretation* for quotations from 'War and Peace in the New Testament' by Victor Paul Furnish in *Interpretation* 38(4) (October 1984); The Most Revd Rowan Williams for quotations from *The Truce of God*; The Catholic University of America Press for quotations from 'The Challenge of Peace: A Historic Peace Church Perspective' by John Howard Yoder in *Peace in a Nuclear Age: The Bishops' Pastoral Letter in Perspective* edited by Charles J. Reid Jr; Oxford University Press for a quotation from *Tranquillitas Ordinis: The Present Failure and Future Promise of American Catholic Thought on War and Peace* by George Weigel © Oxford University Press 1987; Mowbray Continuum for a quotation from *Christianity & War in a Nuclear Age* by Richard Harries; *Hansard* for a quotation from Bishop George Bell's speech to the House of Lords on 9 February 1944; Hodder & Stoughton for quotations from *The Church and the Bomb: Nuclear Weapons and Christian Conscience*; The Merlin Press for quotations from 'War and Murder' by G.E.M. Anscombe and 'Postscript: Counterforce and Countervalue' by Anthony Kenny in *Nuclear Weapons and Christian Conscience* edited by Walter Stein; The Right Revd Richard Harries for quotations from 'The Morality of Nuclear Deterrence' in *What Hope in an Armed World?* edited by Richard Harries; Church House Publishing for a quotation from *Peacemaking in a Nuclear Age* copyright © The Archbishops' Council; Jean Bethke Elshtain for a quotation from *Women and War*; Andrew Chester and CND Publications for 'The Apocalypse and the Nuclear Holocaust' in *In God We Trust* edited by V. Flessati 1986; I.B. Tauris & Co Ltd for a quotation from *The Vision of Islam: The Foundations of Muslim Faith and Practice* by Sachiko Murata and William C. Chittick; HarperCollins Publishers for quotations from *The Koran Interpreted* by Arthur J. Arberry; Oxford University Press for a quotation from 'Politics and War' by Bernard Lewis in *The Legacy of Islam* edited by Joseph Schacht with C.E. Bosworth © Oxford University Press 1974 and 'John Locke and the Case for Toleration' by Maurice Cranston in *On Toleration* edited by Susan Mendus and David Edwards; Edinburgh University Press for quotations from *Islamic Political Thought* by W. Montgomery Watt © W. Montgomery Watt 1968; Vallentine Mitchell & Co for a quotation from *Arab Attitudes to Israel* by Y. Harkabi; John F. Neale for a quotation from *Christian Ethics*, Vol. II by C. Henry Peschke SVD; Darton Longman & Todd Ltd for quotations from *Theological Investigations*, Vol. V by Karl Rahner; and Michael A. Sells for a quotation from 'Bosnia: Some Dimensions of Genocide' in *Religious Studies News* 9(2), 1994.

Further reading

Introductory and general

Astley, J. (2000) *Choosing Life? Christianity and Moral Problems*, London, Darton, Longman & Todd.

Bainton, R. H. (1961) *Christian Attitudes Towards War and Peace*, London, Hodder & Stoughton.

Brown, D. (1983) *Choices: Ethics and the Christian*, Oxford, Blackwell.

Cook, D. (1983) *The Moral Maze: A Way of Exploring Christian Ethics*, London, SPCK.

Crawford, R. (2000) *Can We Ever Kill?*, London, Darton, Longman & Todd.

Freedman, L. (ed.) (1994) *War*, Oxford, Oxford University Press.

Glover, J. (1977, reprinted 1990) *Causing Death and Saving Lives*, Harmondsworth, Penguin.

Glover, J. (1999) *Humanity: A Moral History of the Twentieth Century*, London, Jonathan Cape.

Hauerwas, S. (1984) *The Peaceable Kingdom: A Primer in Christian Ethics*, London, SCM.

Higginson, R. H. (1988) *Dilemmas: A Christian Approach to Moral Decision Making*, London, Hodder & Stoughton.

Jones, R. G. (1984) *Groundwork of Christian Ethics*, London, Epworth.

McDonald, J. I. H. (1995) *Christian Values: Theory and Practice in Christian Ethics Today*, Edinburgh, T & T Clark.

Vardy, P. and Grosch, P. (1994) *The Puzzle of Ethics*, London, HarperCollins.

1 The context: Theology and ethics

Banner, M. (1999) *Christian Ethics and Contemporary Moral Problems*, Cambridge, Cambridge University Press.

Baron, M. W., Pettit, P. and Slote, M. (1997) *Three Methods of Ethics: A Debate*, Oxford, Blackwell.

Birch, B. and Rasmussen, L. (1989) 'The Use of the Bible in Christian

Ethics', in R. P. Hamel and K. R. Himes (eds) *Introduction to Christian Ethics: A Reader*, New York, Paulist, pp. 322–31.

Brunner, E. (1937) *The Divine Imperative: A Study in Christian Ethics*, ET London, Lutterworth.

Copleston, F. (1955) *Aquinas*, Harmondsworth, Penguin, Ch. 5.

Curran, C. E. (1986) *Directions in Fundamental Moral Theology*, Notre Dame, IN, University of Notre Dame Press.

Gill, R. (ed.) (2001) *The Cambridge Companion to Christian Ethics*, Cambridge, Cambridge University Press.

Grenz, S. J. (1997) *The Moral Quest: Foundations of Christian Ethics*, Leicester, Apollos.

Gustafson, J. M. (1981) *Theology and Ethics*, Oxford, Blackwell.

Hoose, B. (ed.) (1998) *Christian Ethics: An Introduction*, London, Cassell.

Hospers, J. (1972) *Human Conduct: Problems of Ethics*, New York, Harcourt Brace Jovanovich.

Keeling, M. (1990) *The Foundations of Christian Ethics*, Edinburgh, T & T Clark.

McDonald, J. I. H. (1993) *Biblical Interpretation and Christian Ethics*, Cambridge, Cambridge University Press.

O'Donovan, O. M. T. (1994) *Resurrection and Moral Order: An Outline for Evangelical Ethics*, Leicester, Apollos.

Ogletree, T. W. (1984) *The Use of the Bible in Christian Ethics*, Oxford, Blackwell.

Rodd, C. S. (ed.) (1995) *New Occasions Teach New Duties? Christian Ethics for Today*, Edinburgh, T & T Clark.

Schnackenburg, R. (1975) *The Moral Teaching of the New Testament*, ET London, Burns & Oates.

Singer, P. (ed.) (1993) *A Companion to Ethics*, Oxford, Blackwell.

Smart, J. J. C. and Williams, B. (1973) *Utilitarianism For and Against*, Cambridge, Cambridge University Press.

Spohn, W. C. (1999) *Go and Do Likewise: Jesus and Ethics*, New York, Continuum.

Waddams, H. (1972) *A New Introduction to Moral Theology*, London, SCM.

White, R. E. O. (1994) *Christian Ethics*, Leominster, Gracewing.

Wogaman, J. P. (1976) *A Christian Method of Moral Judgment*, London, SCM.

2 Peace and pacifism

Bishop, P. (1994) 'New Occasions Teach New Duties? 10: War, Peace-keeping and Terrorism', *Expository Times*, 106, 1, pp. 4–9. (Reprinted in

C. S. Rodd (ed.) (1995) *New Occasions Teach New Duties? Christian Ethics for Today*, Edinburgh, T & T Clark, pp. 129–43.)

Cadoux, C. J. (1919) *The Early Christian Attitude to War: A Contribution to the History of Christian Ethics*, London, Headley Bros.

Cahill, L. S. (1994) *Love Your Enemies: Discipleship, Pacifism and Just War Theory*, Minneapolis, MN, Fortress.

Culliton, J. T. (ed) (1982) *Nonviolence Central to Christian Spirituality: Perspectives from Scripture to the Present*, New York, Edwin Mellen.

Davis, G. S. (1992) *Warcraft and the Fragility of Virtue: An Essay in Aristotelian Ethics*, Moscow, ID, University of Idaho Press.

Egan, E. (1999) *Peace Be with You: Justified Warfare or the Way of Nonviolence*, Maryknoll, New York, Orbis Books.

Furnish, V. P. (1984) 'War and Peace in the New Testament', *Interpretation*, XXXVIII, 4, pp. 363–79.

Hauerwas, S. (1984) *The Peaceable Kingdom: A Primer in Christian Ethics*, London, SCM, pp. 135–51.

Hays, R. B. (1997) *The Moral Vision of the New Testament: A Contemporary Introduction to New Testament Ethics*, Edinburgh, T & T Clark, pp. 317–46.

Hornus, J.-M. (1980) *It Is Not Lawful for Me to Fight: Early Christian Attitudes toward War, Violence, and the State*, Scottdale, PA, Herald.

Lowe, W. (1994) 'Militarism, Evil, and the Reign of God', in R. S. Chopp and M. L. Taylor (eds) *Reconstructing Christian Theology*, Minneapolis, MN, Fortress, pp. 195–219.

MacGregor, G. M. C. (1936) *The New Testament Basis for Pacifism*, London, James Clarke.

Martin, D. (1965) *Pacifism: An Historical and Sociological Study*, London, Routledge.

Martin, D. (1999) 'Christianity, The Church, War – and the WCC', *Modern Believing*, 40, 1, pp. 22–34.

Merton, T. (1996) *Passion for Peace: The Social Essays*, ed. W. H. Shannon, New York, Crossroad.

Phillips, R. L. and Cady, D. L. (1996) *Humanitarian Intervention: Just War vs. Pacifism*, Lanham, Rowman and Littlefield.

Ramsey, P. (1988) *Speak up for Just War or Pacifism: A Critique of the United Methodist Bishops' Pastoral Letter 'In Defense of Creation'*, University Park, University of Pennsylvania Press.

Swartley, W. M. (1992) *The Love of Enemy and Nonretaliation in the New Testament*, Louisville, Westminster/John Knox Press.

Teichman, J. (1986) *Pacifism and the Just War: A Study in Applied Philosophy*, Oxford, Blackwell.

Vaillant, F. (1993) 'Let Us Cease to Compromise with Violence', in B. Wicker (ed.) *Studying War – No More? From Just War to Just Peace*, Kampen, Kok, pp. 170–8.

Weigel, G. (1987) *Tranquillitas Ordinis: The Present Failure and Future Promise of American Catholic Thought on War and Peace*, New York, Oxford University Press.

Williams, R. (1983) *The Truce of God*, London, Collins.

Yoder, J. H. (1986) 'The Challenge of Peace: A Historic Peace Church Perspective', in C. J. Reid, Jr (ed.) *Peace in a Nuclear Age: The Bishops' Pastoral Letter in Perspective*, Washington, DC, The Catholic University of America Press, pp. 273–90.

Yoder, J. H. (1994) *The Politics of Jesus: Vicit Agnus Noster*, Grand Rapids, MI, Eerdmans.

Yoder, J. H. (1998) *The Original Revolution: Essays on Christian Pacifism*, Eugene, OR, Wipf and Stock.

3 The just war and the nuclear option

Anscombe, G. E. M. (1961) 'War and Murder', in W. Stein (ed.) *Nuclear Weapons and Christian Conscience*, London, The Merlin Press, pp. 45–62.

Bailey, S. D. (1987) *War and Conscience in the Nuclear Age*, London, Macmillan.

Bauckham, R. and Elford, R. J. (eds) (1989) *The Nuclear Weapons Debate*, London, SCM.

Church of England Board for Social Responsibility (1982) *The Church and the Bomb: Nuclear Weapons and Christian Conscience*, London, Hodder & Stoughton.

Davies, J. (1995) *The Christian Warrior in the Twentieth Century*, Lewiston, New York, Edwin Mellen.

Decosse, D. E. (ed.) (1992) *But Was it Just? Reflections on the Morality of the Persian Gulf War*, New York, Doubleday.

Finnis, J., Boyle, J. M., Jr and Grisez, G. (1987) *Nuclear Deterrence, Morality and Realism*, Oxford, Oxford University Press.

Goodwin, G. (ed.) (1982) *Ethics and Nuclear Deterrence*, London, Croom Helm.

Harries, R. (1986) *Christianity and War in a Nuclear Age*, London, Mowbray.

Hulett, L. S. (ed.) (1993) *Christianity and Modern Politics*, Berlin, W. de Gruyter.

Moltmann, J. (1990) 'Political Theology and the Ethics of Peace', in L. S.

Rouner (ed.) *Celebrating Peace*, Notre Dame, IN, Notre Dame University Press, pp. 102–17.

National Conference of Catholic Bishops (1983) *The Challenge of Peace: God's Promise and Our Response*, Washington, DC, United States Catholic Conference.

O'Donovan, O. (1989) *Peace and Certainty: A Theological Essay on Deterrence*, Oxford, Oxford University Press.

Ramsey, P. (1961) *War and the Christian Conscience: How Shall Modern War be Conducted Justly?*, Durham, NC, Duke University Press.

Ramsey, P. (1983) *The Just War: Force and Political Responsibility*, Savage, MD, Littlefield, Adams.

Reid, C. J., Jr (1986) *Peace in a Nuclear Age: The Bishops' Pastoral Letter in Perspective*, Washington, DC, The Catholic University of America Press.

Rogers, P. and Dando, M. (1992) *A Violent Peace: Global Security after the Cold War*, London, Brassey's.

Rouner, L. S. (ed.) (1990) *Celebrating Peace*, Notre Dame, IN, Notre Dame University Press.

Santoni, R. E. (1991) 'Nurturing the Institution of War: "Just War" Theory's "Justifications" and Accommodations', in R. A. Hinde (ed.) *The Institution of War*, New York, St Martin's Press, pp. 99–120.

Teichman, J. (1986) *Pacifism and the Just War: A Study in Applied Philosophy*, Oxford, Blackwell.

Walzer, M. (2000) *Just and Unjust Wars: A Moral Argument with Historical Illustrations*, New York, Basic Books.

Wicker, B. (ed.) (1993) *Studying War – No More? From Just War to Just Peace*, Kampen, Kok.

4 Holy wars and holy tolerance

Berger, M. (1962) *The Arab World Today*, London, Weidenfield & Nicolson.

Cohn-Sherbok, D. and El-Alami, D. (2002) *The Palestine-Israel Conflict: A Beginner's Guide*, Oxford, Oneworld.

Cranston, M. (1987) 'John Locke and the Case for Toleration', in S. Mendus and D. Edwards (eds) *On Toleration*, Oxford, Oxford University Press, pp. 101–21.

Davis, G. S. (ed.) (1996) *Religion and Justice in the War Over Bosnia*, London, Routledge.

Declaration of Religious Liberty ('Dignitatis Humanae') (1965) extracts in R. Charles, SJ with D. Maclaren, *The Social Teaching of Vatican II*, Oxford, Plater, 1982, pp. 381–5.

Firestone, R. (1999) *Jihad: The Origin of Holy War in Islam*, Oxford, Oxford University Press.

Goitein, S. D. (1964, 1974) *Jews and Arabs: Their Contacts through the Ages*, New York, Schocken Books.

Griffith, L. (2002) *The War on Terrorism and the Terror of God*, Grand Rapids, MI, Eerdmans.

Haleem, H.; Ramsbotham, O.; Risaluddin, S. and Wicker, B. (eds) (1998) *The Crescent and the Cross: Muslim and Christian Approaches to War and Peace*, Basingstoke, Macmillan.

Harkabi, Y. (1972) *Arab Attitudes to Israel*, ET London, Vallentine, Mitchell.

Hick, J. (1973) *God and the Universe of Faiths*, London, Macmillan, Chs 9 and 10.

Johnson, J. T. (1997) *The Holy War Idea in Western and Islamic Traditions*, University Park, PA, Pennsylvania State University Press.

Johnson, J. T. and Kelsay, J. (eds) (1990) *Cross, Crescent and Sword: The Justification of War in Western and Islamic Tradition*, New York, Greenwood Press.

Kelsay, J. (1993) *Islam and War: A Study in Comparative Ethics*, Louisville, KT, Westminster/John Knox Press.

Kelsay, J. and Johnson, J. T. (eds) (1991) *Just War and Jihad: Historical and Theoretical Perspectives on War and Peace*, New York, Greenwood Press.

Khadduri, M., (1955) *War and Peace in the Law of Islam*, Baltimore, MD, Johns Hopkins Press.

Knight, C. C. (2002) 'Unjust War? The September Attacks and the Attack on Modernity', *Theology*, CV, 826, pp. 255–65.

Lawrence, B. B. (1990) 'Reconsidering "Holy War" (Jihad) in Islam', *Islam and Christian-Muslim Relations*, 1, 2, pp. 261–2.

Lewis, B. (1974) 'Politics of War', in J. Schacht and C. E. Bosworth (eds) *The Legacy of Islam*, Oxford, Oxford University Press, pp. 156–209.

Lewis, B. (1970, 1993) *The Arabs in History*, Oxford, Oxford University Press.

Lewis, B., Pellat, Ch., Schacht, J. (eds) (1965) 'djihad', in *Encyclopaedia of Islam*, 2, Leiden, E. J. Brill, pp. 538–40.

Little, D., Kelsay, J. and Sachedina, A. A. (1988) *Human Rights and the Conflict of Cultures: Western and Islamic Perspectives on Religious Liberty*, Columbia, SC, University of Carolina Press.

Neill, S. (1984) *Crises of Belief: The Christian Dialogue with Faith and No Faith*, London, Hodder & Stoughton.

Norris, H. T. (1993) *Islam in the Balkans: Religion and Society Between Europe and the Arab World*, London, Hurst.

Partner, P. (1997) *God of Battles: Holy Wars of Christianity and Islam*, London, HarperCollins.

Pruthi, R. K. (ed.) (2002) *Encyclopaedia of Jihad*, New Delhi, Anmol, 5 volumes.

Ruston, R. (1993) 'The War of Religions and the Religion of War', in B. Wicker (ed.) *Studying War – No More? From Just War to Just Peace*, Kampen, Kok, pp. 128–41.

Simms, B. (2002) *Unfinest Hour: Britain and the Destruction of Bosnia*, London, Penguin.

Steinberg, J. (1992) 'The Roman Catholic Church and Genocide in Croatia 1941–1945', in D. Wood (ed.) *Christianity and Judaism*, Oxford, Blackwell, pp. 463–80.

Taylor, J. V. (1959) 'Religion: Peace-maker or Peacebreaker', *Islamic Quarterly*, 33, 1, pp. 51–6.

Thomas Aquinas (1959) 'On the Government of Jews', in A. P. D'Entrèves (ed.) *Aquinas: Selected Political Writings*, ET Oxford, Blackwell, pp. 84–95.

Trüger, K.-W. (1990) 'Peace and Islam: In Theory and Practice', *Islam and Christian-Muslim Relations*, 1, 1, pp. 12–24.

Von Grunebaum (1961) *Medieval Islam*, Chicago, University of Chicago Press.

Walzer, M. (1997) *On Toleration*, New Haven, CT, Yale University Press.

Watt, W. M. (1968) *Islamic Political Thought: Basic Concepts*, Edinburgh, Edinburgh University Press, ch. 4.

Wicker, B. (2003) 'Conflict and Martyrdom after 11 September 2001', *Theology*, CVI, 831, pp. 159–67.

Williams, R. (2002) *Writing in the Dust: Reflections on 11ᵗʰ September and its Aftermath*, London, Hodder & Stoughton.

General introductions to Islam

Cohn-Sherbok, D. (ed.) (1991) *Islam in a World of Diverse Faiths*, Basingstoke, Macmillan.

Esack, F. (1999) *On Being a Muslim*, Oxford, Oneworld.

McDermott, M. and Ahsan, M. (1986) *The Muslim Guide: For Teachers, Employers, Community Workers and Social Administrators in Britain*, Leicester, The Islamic Foundation.

Mujtaba, S. and Lari, R. M. (1979) *Western Civilisation Through Muslim Eyes*, ET Huston, TX, Free Islamic Literatures.

Index of subjects

anonymous Christians 82–5
Aquinas and ethics 15–17
Aristotle and ethics 5
ascesis 58

Bible and ethics 2, 13–14, 17–18, 32–3,
    58–60
   see also Jesus and ethics
bluff 55–6
bombing, area/carpet 47–9
Bosnia 85–90
Butler and ethics 5, 15

casuistry 2, 24
categorical imperative 6
church 24–6, 33–4, 38–9, 43–4, 77, 85
Cold War 3
community 24–6
confession, sacrament of 8
conscience 2, 16–17
conscientious objection 42
consequentialist ethics 1–2, 7, 10–15,
    23
costs-benefits 12
covenant 8
crucifixion/cross 2–3, 19–30

Da'wah 96
Decalogue 6
democracy 57
deontological ethics 1, 5–7, 23
double effect 3, 51–3
duty, *see* deontological ethics

ethics 2
ethnic cleansing 85–90
euthanasia 19, 20

flourishing 1
freedom 4, 21, 77–9

genocide 85–90
Good Samaritan 31

Hadith 96
Hajj 95
Haram 93
Helsinki Watch Reports 87
Hijrah 92
Hiroshima 53
Hitler 47–50
holy war 62–72

idealism, moral 18–19
Imam Ali 71–2
individual worth 80–1
'Isa 91
Isaac 91
Ishmael 91
Islam 95
Islamic/Muslim ethics 4, 62–75, 90–6
Israel, Ancient 32–3

Jesus and ethics 2, 5, 9, 27–33, 35–7, 39
Jewish ethics 56
Jewish-Christian relations 75–6, 84
jihad 4, 62–72, 95
jizya 74
Judas 36
just war 3, 9, 43–61
    criteria of 3, 44–5

Kant and ethics 6
kingdom of God 37, 39
Koran, *see* Qur'an and ethics
Kosovo 86

law 50
    see also deontological ethics
Law, the 27–9
Liberation Theology 9

liberty 8
love 2–3, 8–9, 14–15, 27, 29, 31, 39
loyalty 57
Luther and ethics 21

Madinah/Medina 92
magisterium 7
Makkah/Mecca 91–2
Mi'raj 92
mistakes, moral 17
Moral Majority 59
morality and Christianity/religion 1,
    5–10
Moses/*Musa* 91
    see also Decalogue
mosque 64
Mountain Wreath 86–8
Muhammad 91–4
mujahada 63
Muslim 95
Muslim-Christian relations 67–8, 72,
    85–90
Muslim-Jewish relations 67–8, 72–5
mutually assured destruction 55

Nabi 90
Nagasaki 53
narrative 9
natural law 1, 5
neighbour 31, 39
New Testament, *see* Bible and ethics
non-combatants 19–20, 45, 50–6
norms, moral 17–20
nuclear deterrence/nuclear war 3, 43–61
    and just war criteria 46

objectivity, moral 16
Old Testament, *see* Bible and ethics
other faiths
    and Christianity 79–85
    approaches to 79–82

pacifism 2, 27–42
pacifist churches 38
Paul and ethics 28, 36
peace 28, 35–7
peace, kiss of 34
Plato and ethics 5
pleasure 11–12
pride 82

Protestant ethics 5–7, 9–10

Qur'an and ethics 4, 62, 64–6, 71, 74–5

reconciliation, *see* confession
religion and morality 1, 5–10
religions, theology of 4
    see also other faiths
repentance 59
Revelation, Book of 58–60
revolution 45
Roman Catholic ethics 5, 8–10, 16–17,
    18–19, 40–2, 51, 53
rules 10, 24
    see also deontological ethics

Salat/Salah 94
Sawm 94–5
Shahadah 93–4, 95
Shahid-a 95
Shar'iah 93
Shi'a 93
Shirk 95
sin 18–19, 21–2
    original sin 83
Stoicism 5
Sunni 93

teleological ethics 5, cf. 23
Temple cleansing 30
testing, moral 25–6
tolerance/toleration 4, 72–3, 76–9
truce of God 33

Ummah 93
United Nations 41, 90
usury 75–6
utilitarianism 2, 6–7, 10–13, 23
    see also consequentialist ethics

Vatican II / Second Vatican Council 8, 40,
    78–9
violence 25
virtue 5

women and war 58
World War II 47–50

zakat 71–2, 94
Zionism 41

Index of names

Abraham 91, 95
Aga Khan, the 93
Ahsan, M. 105
Al-Jiyar, A. 74
Ambrose, St 44
Andric, I. 88–9
Anscombe, G. E. M. 52–3, 102
Aquinas, St Thomas 15–17, 75–6, 105
Arberry, A. J. 64, 66, 92
Arendt, H. 58
Aristotle 5
Arthur, L. 20
Astley, J. 99
Augustine, St 8, 17, 43–4

Bailey, S. D. 102
Bainton, R. H. 99
Banner, M. 99
Baron, M. W. 99
Barth, K. 7, 10
Bauckham, R. 102
Becket, St Thomas 34
Bell, G. 47–50
Bentham, J. 6, 11–12
Berger, M. 72, 103
Birch, B. 17–18, 99–100
Bishop, P. 100–1
Bonhoeffer, D. 7, 22
Bosworth, C. E. 67, 104
Boyle, J. M., Jr 102
Brown, D. 5–10, 14–15, 99
Brunner, E. 7, 100
Bundy, M. 55
Butler, J. 5, 15

Cadoux, C. J. 101
Cady, D. L. 101
Cahill, L. S. 101
Caiaphas 37
Charles, R. 103

Cheshire, L. 55
Chester, A. 58–60
Chesterton, G. K. 34
Chittick, W. C. 62–4
Chopp, R. S. 101
Church of England Board for Social
    Responsibility 102
Churchill, W. 49
Clements, K. 57
Clinton, W. (President) 89
Cohn-Sherbok, D. 103, 105
Constantine (Emperor) 9, 43
Cook, D. 99
Copleston, F. C. 16–17, 100
Cranston, M. 76–8, 103
Crawford, R. 99
Culliton, J. T. 101
Curran, C. E. 2, 18–20, 26, 100

D'Entrèves, A. P. 75–6, 105
Dando, M. 103
Davies, J. 102
Davis, G. S. 101, 103
Dawood, N. J. 64–6
Decosse, D. E. 102
Djilas, M. 87
Dunstan, G. R. 1

Edwards, D. 76–8, 103
Egan, E. 101
El-Alami, D. 103
Elford, R. J. 102
Elshtain, J. B. 58
Esack, F. 105

Farmer, H. H. 30
Finnis, J. 102
Firestone, R. 104
Fletcher, J. 8
Freedman, L. 99

Furnish, V. P. 32–3, 101

Gabriel 94
General Synod of the Church of England
    57–8
Gill, R. 1, 100
Glover, J. 99
Glubb, J. B. (Glubb Pasha) 68
Goitein, S. D. 73, 104
Goodwin, G. 102
Grenz, S. J. 100
Griffith, L. 104
Grisez, G. 102
Grosch, P. 99
Gustafson, J. M. 8, 100

Haleem, H. 104
Hamel, R. P. 17–18, 100
Häring, B. 8
Harkabi, Y. 72–5, 104
Harries, R. 3, 43–7, 54–7, 102
Hauerwas, S. 3, 9, 23–6, 99, 101
Hays, R. B. 101
Helsinki Watch Reports 87
Hick, J. 104
Higginson, R. H. 10–13, 20–22, 99
Himes, K. R. 17–18, 100
Hinde, R. A. 103
Hoose, B. 1, 100
Hornus, J.-M. 101
Hospers, J. 100
Hulett, L. S. 102

Ibrahim, *see* Abraham
Ipgrave, M. 90–96
Ishmael 95

Jesus 2, 5, 8–9, 25–33, 35–7, 39, 91–2
John XXIII, (Pope) 18–19
Johnson, J. T. 104
Jones, R. G. 99

Kahn, H. 54
Kant, I. 1, 6, 8
Karadzic, R. 89
Keeling, M. 100
Kelsay, J. 104
Kenny, A. 53–4
Khadduri, M 70, 104
Knight, C. C. 104
Knox, J. 31–2

Lari, R. M. 69–72, 105
Lawrence, B. B. 104
Lazar (Prince) 86–7
Leon, P. 82
Lewis, B. 67, 73, 104
Little, D. 104
Loades, A. 90–6
Locke, J. 76–8
Lowe, W. 101
Luther, M. 2, 21–2

McCormick, R. A. 19–20
McDermott, M. 105
McDonald, J. I. H. 99–100
MacGregor, G. M. C. 2, 27–30, 101
Maclaren, D. 103
McNamara, R. 53–4
Marcion 27
Martin, D. 101
Mary 91–2
Matheson, P. 34
Melanchthon, P. 21
Mendus. S. 76–8, 103
Merton, T. 101
Mill, J. S. 2, 6, 8, 11–12
Milosevic, S. 87
Mladic, R. 89
Moltmann, J. 102–3
Moses 91
Muhammad 91–5
Mujtaba, S. 69–72, 105
Murata, S. 62–4

National Conference of Catholic Bishops
    103
Neill, S. 104
Niebuhr, R. 3
Nikolaj, M. 89
Njegos (aka Petar II, Prince Bishop) 86–9
Norris, H. T. 104
Nygren, A. 8

O'Connor, J. (Bishop) 40
O'Donovan, O. 100, 103
Ogletree, T. W. 13–14, 100

Partner, P. 104
Paskins, B. 56
Paton, H. J. 1
Paul, St 28
Pellat, Ch. 104

Peschke, C. H. 78–9
Petar II, Prince Bishop, *see* Njegos
Pettit, P. 99
Phillips, R. L. 101
Plato 5
Pruthi, R. K. 105

Quinn, P. L. 1

Rahner, K. 82–5
Raiser, K. 61
Ramsbotham, O. 104
Ramsey, P. 2–3, 8, 30–2, 55, 101, 103
Rasmussen, L. 17–18, 99–100
Reid, C. J., Jr 38–9, 102–3
Risaluddin, S. 104
Roberts, T. A. 15
Rodd, C. S. 5, 101
Rogers, P. 103
Rouner, L. S. 102–3
Ruston, R. 105

Sachedina, A. A. 104
Santoni, R. E. 103
Schacht, J. 67, 104
Schnackenburg, R. 100
Sells, M. A. 85–90
Shannon, W. H. 101
Simms, B. 105
Singer, P. 1, 100
Slote, M. 99
Smart, J. J. C. 2, 100
Socrates 11
Spohn, W. C. 100
Stein, W. 52–6, 102

Steinberg, J. 105
Swartley, W. M. 101

Tabbara, A. 75
Taliaferro, C. 1
Taylor, J. 56
Taylor, J. V. 105
Taylor, M. L. 101
Teichman, J. 101, 103
Thielicke, H. 10, 20–2, 26
Trüger, K.-W. 105

Vaglieri, L. V. 72
Vaillant, F. 102
van Duser, H. P. 31–2
Vardy, P. 99
von Grunebaum, G. E. 73, 105

Waddams, H. 100
Walzer, M. 103, 105
Warren, M. 79–82
Watt, W. M. 68–9, 105
Weigel, G. 40–2, 102
White, R. E. O. 100
Wicker, B. 102–5
Williams, B. 2, 20, 100
Williams, R. 33–7, 102, 105
Wogaman, J. P. 100
Wood, D. 105
Wordsworth, W. 11

Yoder, J. H. 2, 9, 38–9, 102

Zahn, G. 40
Zhirinovsky, V. 89